CAREER CHOICES

A Guide for Teens and Young Adults:
Who Am I?
What Do I Want?
How Do I Get It?

Written by Mindy Bingham and Sandy Stryker
Edited by Tanja Easson

Illustrated by Itoko Maeno, Janice Blair, and Diana Lackner

Academic Innovations, Santa Barbara, California

This book belongs to _____

Started on _____

Completed on _____

I dedicate this work to _____

Copies of this book, along with an *Instructor's and Counselor's Guide* and a consumable workbook, are available directly from the publisher. Call Academic Innovations at (800) 967-8016 for ordering and shipping information.

Fifth Edition © 2011 by Melinda Bingham
Fourth Edition © 2009 by Melinda Bingham
Third Edition © 2003 by Melinda Bingham
Second Edition © 2000 by Melinda Bingham
First Edition © 1990 by Melinda Bingham and Sandy Stryker

Library of Congress Catalog Card Number: 90-81785

ISBN 978-1-878787-41-1 Hardcover
ISBN 978-1-878787-38-1 Softcover

Published by Academic Innovations
(800) 967-8016   FAX (800) 967-4027
www.academicinnovations.com
support@academicinnovations.com

Manufactured in the United States of America

25   24   23   22   21

We have taken the privilege of substituting certain words in the quotations cited here ("person" instead of "man," "people" instead of "men") to make them more inclusive, with the certainty that, had they been said today, this is how they would have been stated.

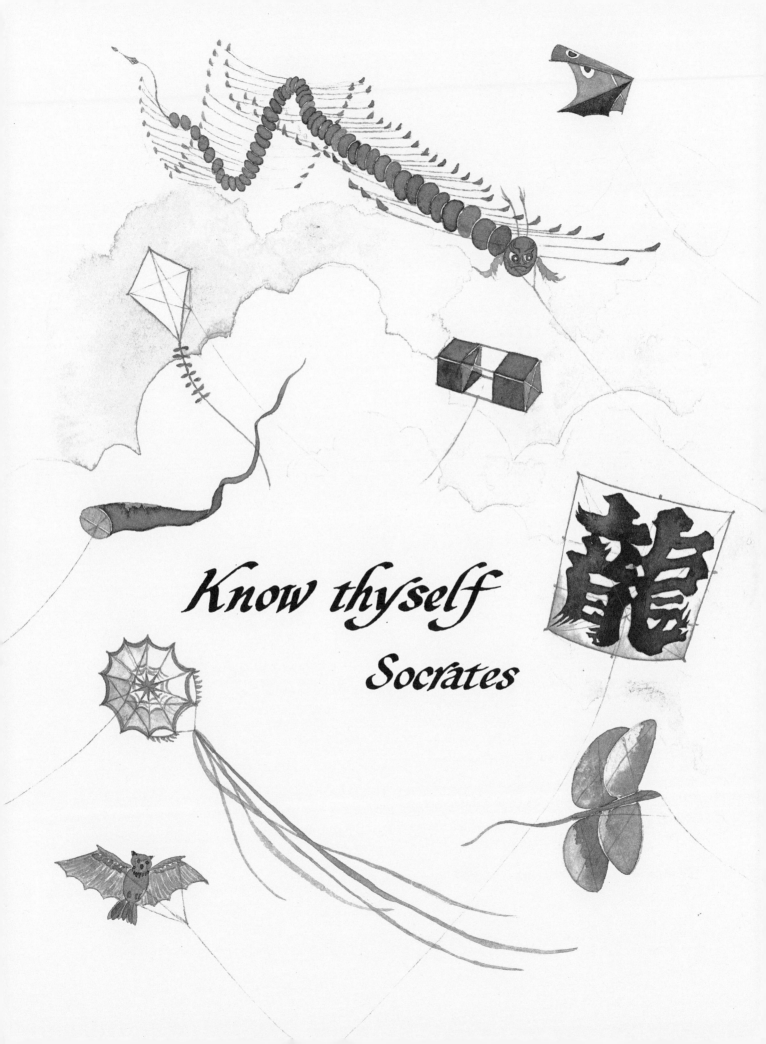

Know thyself

Socrates

CONTENTS

*T*he assignment was puzzling in light of the fact that they were supposed to start a unit on career planning today. But Mr. Ziegfeld refused to elaborate. "Bring me something that flies," he'd said. As the students began to drift into the classroom, it was clear that they had interpreted the assignment in a variety of ways.

Beautifully decorated kites mingled with bunches of balloons. Model planes ran the gamut from Wilbur and Orville Wright's first craft to the latest supersonic jets. There were helicopters and spaceships, gliders and seaplanes. Working models of a blimp and a hot air balloon hovered near the ceiling. Several superheroes were represented, with Superman and Wonder Woman apparently the favorites. Someone dressed like Charles Lindbergh chatted with an Amelia Earhart look-alike. Chuck Yeager, Sally Ride, and John Glenn impersonators joined the group. A pet parakeet's song was drowned out by the coos from a box of pigeons.

Finally, Mr. Ziegfeld called the class to order. Students took their seats, anxious to learn what this was all about. "Okay," he said. "Let's talk about career planning."

"Wait a minute," said Superman. "Aren't you going to explain the assignment? What does all this flying business have to do with choosing a career?"

"Oh, that," Mr. Ziegfeld replied. "You'd probably figure it out soon enough, but I guess I can fill you in now. It's really quite simple. Deciding what to do with your life is a lot like learning to fly. I just wanted you to see that there are lots of ways to do it. Take a look around the room and hold on to this image.

"What's right for Charles Lindbergh will probably not suit Sally Ride. Yet both of them are heroes. Some people take direct flights. Others stop at points of interest along the way. The pace of the journey is an individual matter as well. That's why it's important to know who you are and what you want.

"You won't necessarily choose your life's career in this class. But you will learn a process that you can use again and again, as you adjust to the future and keep making plans. Once you learn this, you'll be able to proceed more easily, no matter what you decide to do.

"Now, let's get started. Up and away!"

Visit http://www.my10yearplan.com where contents and data from pages displaying this logo can be entered into this *optional* web-based enhancement for tracking your plans.

Visit http://www.careerchoices.com when you see this logo:

You'll find valuable Internet resources, calculators, and charts that will enhance your understanding of the topics found on that page.

CHAPTER ONE

Envisioning Your Future

How do you define success?

Personal success is simply the fulfillment
of what makes you happiest.
—Anonymous

Vision is the art of seeing the invisible.
—Jonathan Swift

Section One:
WHO AM I?

APOLO GETS THE MAGIC POTION

One day, Apolo Ohno noticed an old woman attempting to cross the street against heavy traffic. He took the woman's arm and guided her safely to the other side. "Thank you, young man," she said in a thin, wobbly voice. "I want to give you something for your trouble." With that, she reached into her pocket and pulled out a small flask of purple powder that looked as though it had been kept there for years. "What is that?" Apolo asked. "It is my magic potion," she said. "Dissolve a teaspoon of this powder in a glass of soda at 3 o'clock on a Friday afternoon, and it will make you a speed skating star. You will be able to race through curves tighter and faster than any other skater. I've been saving the powder for myself but, because of my arthritis, it's beginning to look as though I won't make the U.S. Olympic speed skating team. Here, do as I tell you."

"Okay," Apolo said enthusiastically.

SALLY WINS THE ASTRO-LOTTERY

Sally Ride was working a crossword puzzle and watching "Jeopardy" one evening when her phone rang. "Congratulations," said the voice on the line, "your name has just been picked from twenty million entries to be the first woman astronaut in America! What do you think of that?" "Gee, it sounds great," said Sally. "Yes, Sally," the voice continued, "you are our lucky winner. You'll be flown as our guest to the luxury astronaut training center in beautiful Houston, Texas, where you will learn space secrets and survival techniques from the experts. Then it'll be off to sunny Cape Canaveral, where you'll blast off into space as millions of people around the world watch and cheer. Your prize also includes the regulation space suit, the freeze-dried gourmet dinners, and assurance that your name will go down in history! What do you say to that, Sally Ride?" "Wow," said Sally.

OPRAH GETS DISCOVERED

Oprah Winfrey got on a downtown bus to go shopping one Saturday. The bus was crowded, and she accidentally stepped on the foot of a man sitting near the front. "Excuse me," she said. The man looked at her. "Would you say that again?" he asked. "Excuse me?" said Oprah. "That's it! People, this is the one!" the man exclaimed. "This is our star!" As he made his announcement, a dozen people jumped up from seats further back in the bus. A camera crew descended on Oprah with microphones and glaring lights. Someone from make-up began highlighting her cheekbones. A costumer told Oprah she'd be stunning in chartreuse. "Wait a minute," Oprah demanded. "What's this all about?" "You're going to be the star of our new talk show," the first man told her. "You'll have your own production company. And you'll make some movies, too. The job pays about 75 million dollars a year. How does that sound?" "Sounds good to me," said Oprah.

BARACK FINDS A JOB

One day, while vacationing in Washington, D.C., Barack Obama saw a sign in the White House window. "Help Wanted," it read. Since he was between jobs at the time, Barack decided to check it out. "We're looking for the next President of the United States," the woman in the office told him. "You have to be an American citizen, and you must be over thirty-five years of age." "That's me," said Barack. "Do I get the job?" "I don't see why not," the woman said. "Of course, you'll have to relocate. Would you mind living in the White House?" "Well, I don't know. Could I think about it for a day or two and get back to you?" "Sure. Take your time. No pressure."

11

VISION + ENERGY = SUCCESS

You can safely assume that there is not one kernel of truth in any of the preceding stories. Successful people do not depend on luck or magic to get what they want. Nor do they let others make their career choices for them. Most people who are successful in their work don't just *find* a job. They *make* one. They have a *vision* of what they would like to do, how they would like to use their minds, talents, and interests. And they have the *energy* to make their dreams come true. They believe in their vision.

Vision and energy (or action) are the two most important elements in getting what you want from life. Your vision of what you'd like to do or be, or how you'd like to live, will help you know when you've succeeded. A goal is like a compass that will help keep you on track. And your energy or actions will take you, step by step, to the realization of your vision.

It is essential to have both elements. Vision without action is just daydreaming. Alone, it won't get you anywhere. Undirected action is equally useless. It leads only to exhaustion and frustration. Together, though, they are a dynamic duo. And they can work for you, no matter what your goal. (Not everyone can—or wants to—be a superstar. You need to have your own definition of success. More on that later in this chapter.)

What do you think are the real stories behind the successful people we talked about on the preceding pages? For the following exercises, write a statement that you feel might reflect his or her vision. Then list some actions they may have taken to realize their goal. Apolo Ohno's chart, for example, might look something like this:

Apolo Ohno

Vision: To be a champion short track speed skater, someone who brings something new to the ice.

Actions in school and work: Throughout junior high, high school, and college, train, train, train; seek out good coaching; watch and analyze top speed skaters; keep up grades to remain eligible to compete; stay healthy.

Actions at work: As a competitive skater, train, train, train; maintain health.

Complete charts for the following individuals.

Sally Ride

Vision: _____

Actions in school: _____

Actions at work: _____

Oprah Winfrey

Vision: _____

Actions in school: _____

Actions at work: _____

Barack Obama

Vision: _____

Actions in school: _____

Actions at work: _____

Envisioning *Your* Future

What about you? Do you have a vision for your own future? You need to begin imagining one, if you don't. It's an important first step. Once you have a vision, you start expecting to realize it. What you expect for yourself tends to become what you get. So imagine a *positive* future for yourself.

Sit quietly, close your eyes, and imagine your ideal career. What kind of setting are you in? What tasks are you performing? Are you working alone or with others? How do you feel about yourself? Describe your vision in as much detail as possible.

_____

_____

_____

_____

_____

_____

_____

_____

_____

Was that a difficult exercise for you? Don't worry about it if it was. The rest of this book is designed to help you begin to clarify who you are, what you want, and what you need to do to get it. So keep reading!

Why People Work

People work for many reasons, but, basically, they work to bring personal meaning and satisfaction to themselves, as well as benefits to society. All human beings have a need to work, to do, and to become someone through that process. According to Kenneth B. Hoyt, known as the "father of career education," we work to "discover both *who* we are and *why* we are."

☐ *Of course, people also work for survival.* In early history, that meant —literally—bringing home the bacon (or the wooly mammoth), gathering fruits and grains, and finding shelter from the elements. Today the transaction is less direct. People work for *money,* which they use to fulfill the same basic needs. But then, you probably already knew that. You may be less aware, however, of some of the *other* reasons people go to work each day. The following come from Dr. Jay B. Rohrlich's book, *Work and Love: The Crucial Balance.*

☐ *People work to define themselves.* Ask most people who they are and they will respond with their occupation: "I'm a mail carrier," "I'm a software designer," "I'm a teacher," and so on. It may be just as accurate to say "I'm an emotional person" or "I'm very creative." But, somehow, statements like these seem more ambiguous. They provide less concrete information. Being able to provide a job title or a list of accomplishments makes us feel more *real* to ourselves and others.

☐ *People work to have a sense of security.* Many people find it difficult to get all the love or approval they need from their relationships with friends and family. For them, work can be a constant source of security and pleasure. They may not know what kind of mood they will find their spouse in on any given night. But they can be fairly certain that their work will be the same.

☐ *People work for self-respect, or to feel competent and powerful.* It isn't always easy to feel powerful in the world. Some people will always be more powerful than you are. Discrimination based on sex or race is real, and robs its victims of the feeling that they can direct the course of their lives. But doing a particular job well gives a worker a sense of control and responsibility that adds greatly to his or her self-respect.

☐ *People work to conquer time.* We are aware from an early age that our time on earth is limited. The days that pass simply vanish. One way we can "conquer" time is to fill each day with achievements or accomplishments. Over time, these experiences become a real and lasting part of what we see ourselves to be.

☐ *People work to measure their self-worth.* Working is one way of "keeping score," of seeing how we stack up in comparison to others. Who is the most accomplished? Who got the award or promotion? Who earned the respect of the group? Who makes the most money? These are all ways we use to measure our self-worth. We feel better about ourselves when we succeed at a *difficult* task than we do when we accomplish something easy. We also tend to place importance on public recognition: the more lives you touch, the longer you may be remembered.

What are your motivations? Why do you work, whether it's at school, at home, or at a job? Prioritize the previous statements by placing a "1" in the box next to the statement that resonates most with your feelings about work. Continue to score each item, with "6" being what you find least matches your personal drives. This basic understanding of why you work and what it brings to you may help you later as you examine your possible career choices.

In the long run, though, true job satisfaction comes only from inside. You are the final judge of your own achievement. Whether you make a fortune or just a living is less important than knowing that you made a contribution and that you did your job well.

Everybody Works

Whether you currently earn money from a job or not, you are a worker. You are probably a student. Chances are you do chores at home. Perhaps you are an athlete or a musician, a computer whiz or a video fanatic, a cook or a gardener. For the purpose of this exercise, consider all your studies, tasks, and hobbies as work.

Think about a typical "working day," one in which you spent time on most of your "jobs." List the tasks and activities you performed below. Make your list as complete as you can.

_____

_____

_____

Based on that list, how would you define your jobs? Write your titles on the following lines.

I am a _____

_____

_____

What would be your accomplishments at the end of the day (an English paper, a clean room, a solved problem, and so on)? List them below.

_____

_____

_____

Which accomplishments are most satisfying? _____

_____

How do they make you feel about yourself? _____

_____

Do your feelings relate to any of the reasons people work listed on the previous page? Which ones?

_____

_____

Defining Success

According to the dictionary, success is "the achievement of something desired, planned, or attempted." Since your desires and plans are very personal and are not exactly like anyone else's, you will need to define success for yourself.

This is not an easy thing to do in our society. Success is often equated with wealth and fame, luxurious homes and fancy cars. These outward displays may *look like* success to others, but they do not make those who possess them *feel* successful. The feeling of success comes only when *you achieve* what is *most important to you*. True success is a personal feeling, not a public display.

What does success mean to you? What would make you feel that you are a successful human being? In addition to thinking about what you do, contemplate the type of person you want to be.

Other people have made their opinions known as well. We've listed some of them below. Do any of them match your definition? Indicate whether you strongly agree, agree, are not sure, disagree, or strongly disagree with each statement.

	Strongly Agree	Agree	Not Sure	Disagree	Strongly Disagree
Money, achievement, fame, and success are important, but they are bought too dearly when acquired at the cost of health. — Anonymous					
It's great to be great, but it's better to be human. — Will Rogers					
Nothing succeeds like excess. — Oscar Wilde					
Success is a journey, not a destination. — Ben Sweetland					
The fastest way to succeed is to look as if you're playing by other people's rules, while quietly playing by your own. — Michael Korda					
She could not separate success from peace of mind. The two must go together... — Daphne Du Maurier, *Mary Anne*					
All of us are born for a reason, but all of us don't discover why. Success in life has nothing to do with what you gain in life or accomplish for yourself. It's what you do for others. — Danny Thomas					
I've never sought success in order to get fame and money; it's the talent and the passion that count in success. — Ingrid Bergman					

	Strongly Agree	Agree	Not Sure	Disagree	Strongly Disagree
The two leading recipes for success are building a better mousetrap and finding a bigger loophole. — Edgar A. Shoaff					
Success is something to enjoy—to flaunt! Otherwise, why work so hard to get it? — Isobel Lennart, *Funny Girl*					
Success is knowing what your values are and living in a way consistent with your values. — Danny Cox					
Success can only be measured in terms of distance traveled... — Mavis Gallant					
If at first you don't succeed, you are running about average. — M.H. Anderson					
I think success has no rules, but you can learn a great deal from failure. — Jean Kerr, *Mary, Mary*					
Success can make you go one of two ways. It can make you a *prima donna,* or it can smooth the edges, take away the insecurities, let the nice things come out. — Barbara Walters					
Six essential qualities that are the key to success: Sincerity, personal integrity, humility, courtesy, wisdom, charity. — Dr. William Menninger					
The people who try to do something and fail are infinitely better than those who try to do nothing and succeed. — Lloyd Jones					
The wealthy man is the man who is much, not the one who has much. — Karl Marx					
Winning isn't everything—it's the only thing. — Vince Lombardi					
Only those who dare to fail greatly can ever achieve greatly. — Robert F. Kennedy					
If at first you don't succeed, try, try again. Then give up. There's no use being a fool about it. — W. C. Fields					
I'm opposed to millionaires, but it would be dangerous to offer me the position. — Mark Twain					

19

Making Career Choices

Later in the book, you will learn a technique that will help you make good decisions in most situations. For now, though, as you begin making choices about your future career, try to be aware of the decision-making patterns you use most often. Some of them work better than others. Some of them don't work at all. Do you recognize yourself in any of the following stories?

ERIC has a tendency toward wishful thinking. He concentrates on the outcome that seems most attractive to him. But he pays little attention to the risks involved, or the probability of his wish coming true. Eric has decided to be a professional tennis player, even though he's not willing to practice. Last spring he was cut from the school's tennis team.

LOUISA is an escape artist. She takes pride in determining the worst thing that could happen in any situation. And, even when there is little chance of that outcome, she chooses a safe alternative. Although Louisa is a straight A student in math, she is afraid she wouldn't do as well in that subject in college. She'd rather be an engineer, but she's decided to major in elementary education.

MAGGIE likes to play it safe. She knows she could be successful as an insurance agent, so she plans to follow that course. Really, though, she'd rather be a politician.

WADE is impulsive. He makes decisions without giving them too much thought. He's thinking of being a flight attendant because he likes the way they dress.

ANDY usually leaves things to fate. He plans to hitch a ride to California after graduation, just to see what happens.

ELENA is compliant. She usually lets someone else make her decisions. Her parents think she should become a computer programmer, so she probably will.

HAROLD procrastinates. He puts off decisions until the last minute. He plans to think about his future after graduation.

YOKO agonizes over every decision. She examines each alternative so closely — and so repeatedly — that she never seems able to make up her mind. She says she wants to interview several dozen more people before selecting a career path.

ARTURO makes decisions intuitively. Some things just feel right, he says. He's always liked the idea of being a wildlife biologist, but he isn't exactly sure what they do.

KENISHA has a rational approach to making decisions. She considers the alternatives, the pros and cons of each, and the likelihood of succeeding before making her choice. She is interested in technology and sees a bright future in computer-related careers, so she plans to train for a job in that field.

Which of these patterns do you use most often? Explain.

_____

_____

Your Definition of Success

Write your own definition of success here:

_____

_____

_____

_____

_____
your name

Throughout this book we will be talking about success. As you read about and ponder this concept, make sure to keep **your own definition** in mind.

There Are Jobs . . . and There Are Careers

Although we often use the terms interchangeably, there is a difference between a *job* and a *career*. A job is a particular task or undertaking. It may be paid or unpaid. You will, undoubtedly, have many jobs during your lifetime.

But you will only have one career. Your career encompasses *all* of your life's work. You have already begun your career. The work you have done so far will help determine where you go from here. Future occupations grow out of past experiences. That is why people speak of career *development*. The path may not always be obvious, but the connections are there. So the choices you make now are important.

Making choices that are right for you is what this book is all about. Before you choose what you want, however, you need to know who you are. That is a subject we will tackle in the next chapter.

What lies behind us and what lies
before us are small matters compared
to what lies within us.
—Ralph Waldo Emerson

Self-trust is the first secret of success.
—Ralph Waldo Emerson

CHAPTER TWO

Your Personal Profile

Getting what you want starts with knowing who you are.

Section One:
WHO AM I?

It was career night at Central High. When Letitia arrived, she found her friend, James, standing outside the gym, looking bewildered. "I didn't expect to find a scene like this," said James. The gym was packed with representatives from dozens of colleges and vocational schools. All branches of the armed forces were represented. And there were prospective employers and people working in a wide variety of careers.

"Isn't it great?" said Letitia. "Every one of those people stands for a possible future, a different way of life! But I guess it could be confusing. It's a good thing we have some ideas about what we want to do."

James cleared his throat and stared at his shoes.

"You do have some ideas, don't you, James?"

"Oh, sure," he replied. "My parents think it would be good for me to enlist in the army for a couple years. And Mr. Johnson, my chemistry teacher, thinks I should go into engineering. He wants me to talk to the admissions officer from his university. Of course, a lot of my friends are going to City College, and that might be fun."

"Yes, but what do you think? What kind of future do you want? You're the one who's going to be living there, you know. Have you considered who you are and what you want?"

"What's there to think about? I'm my parents' son and my friends' friend. I go to high school. I hang out. I'm just me. And who are you, if I may ask?"

"Well, I have thought about it," said Letitia. "In a lot of ways, I'm like you and my other friends. But people are like snowflakes or fingerprints—no two are the same. And it seems to me that it's the differences that make life interesting. We have to consider those things when we plan our lives.

"For example, I enjoy being on the debate team. I love to argue and discuss and try to persuade people, even though most of my friends think that kind of thing is boring. I'm also really interested in civil rights. So I'm thinking about being a lawyer, maybe even running for Congress someday. And those things, James, are all part of who I am."

Letitia has a head start on her friend, but it's not too late for James to consider who he is and what he wants to do. This is a process that can start at any time—and should continue throughout life.

Learning about yourself is a little like painting a picture. When you are very young, you have little more than a sketch—who takes care of you, what you like to eat, what you like to play with. As you grow and change, you learn more and more about yourself and begin to develop a vivid self-portrait. But the portrait is never complete. Some things will change. Many details will be added.

It's important, though, to keep a sort of running tab: "Who am I now? What's important to me at this point in my life? What do I do well? What do I most enjoy?" Your answers to these questions will help you make the decisions that will lead to a satisfying short-term future. By asking them again and again, you will be better able to make the necessary changes and adjustments that lead to a fulfilling life.

You may be tempted to rely on Internet-based or computerized interest surveys. After all, you can complete these in an hour or two and you "magically" get the answer to one of your most important questions—what career(s) match your interests and needs. But there are compelling reasons for you to not take this shortcut. You'll see as you work through this book that choosing a career is complex and multi-dimensional. In the next eleven chapters you'll be evaluating data and feelings that only you can assess.

These feelings and realities will change over the course of your life. Knowing the decision-making process so you can re-evaluate as needed, you'll have a stronger sense of direction and a better handle on your own career options. Then when opportunities or challenges present themselves, you'll be ready to confidently take action to keep yourself and your career on track with your own personal desires and requirements.

So, where do you start? The following exercise should help.

Write your name in the center of the chart, then add as many words as you can that describe your own passions, values, strengths, and so forth.

As you fill out your chart, keep in mind that everyone has many different sides. Don't worry if some of your answers seem incompatible with others. Remember, too, that it's natural to want to "belong." Because you want to be like your peers, you may try to deny interests or abilities that are not shared with your friends. But for this exercise—for your own sake—try to be complete and honest.

Don't get frustrated if you have a hard time completing your chart at this time. It will get easier as you work through this chapter. For now, do your best. Use a pencil so you can make any necessary changes as you go along.

Here are some short definitions to help you:

Passions: A passion is something you feel very strongly about, something for which you have boundless enthusiasm. You might be passionate about music, sports, art, computers, horses, cars, gardening, politics, the beach, marching bands, penguins—you name it. The happiest people are often those who find a way to incorporate their passions into their career. These are the people you'll hear say things like, "I can't believe they pay me to do this."

Values: Your values are those qualities or things that are most important in your life. Some people may value family or security, while others place more importance on adventure or power. You might value beauty, knowledge, social justice, or independence. Your career and life choices should be compatible with your values if they are to bring true satisfaction.

Personality traits and strengths: Are you tactful? Bold? Sociable? Quiet? Thoughtful? Energetic? Funny? Sympathetic? Inquisitive? Reserved? Dramatic? Intelligent? List as many traits as you can.

Skills and aptitudes: What have you learned? What comes easily for you? Do you have a special talent for anything in particular? Are you good at working with your hands? Solving problems? Working with people?

Roles: Your roles are the different parts you play in your life. Most of these are temporary, though some can go on for many years. Right now, you are probably a son or daughter, a student, a friend. You might also be an employee, a sister or brother, a girlfriend or boyfriend, and so on.

Occupations and vocations: Here we mean both work you do for pay (occupations) and recreational activities (vocations). For example, you might be a grocery clerk, babysitter, flute player, cook, ballet dancer, skateboarder, or basketball player.

Your Personal Profile

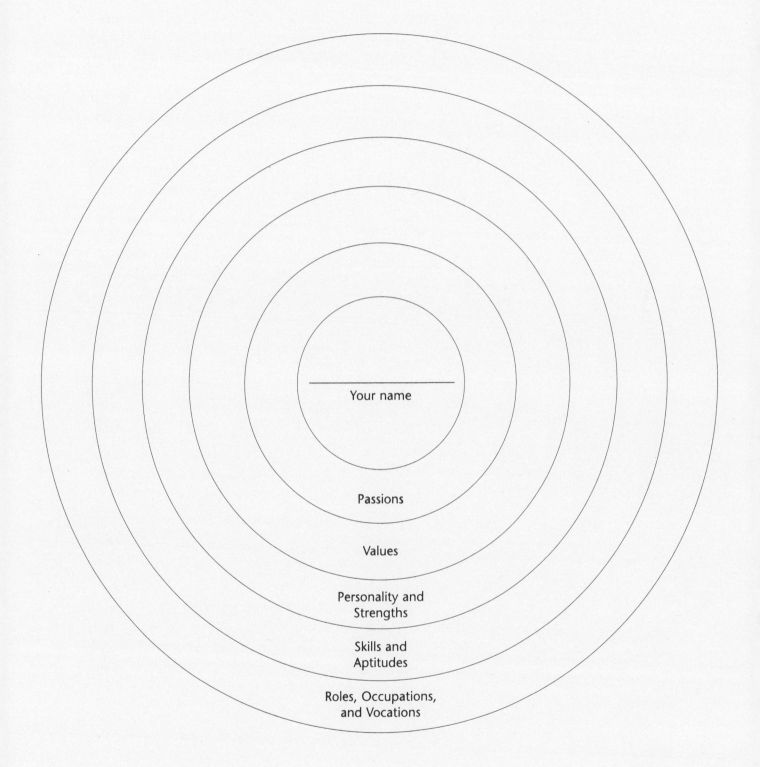

_____
Your name

Passions

Values

Personality and
Strengths

Skills and
Aptitudes

Roles, Occupations,
and Vocations

Back at the gym, Letitia had just finished discussing law school admission requirements with a representative from the state university when James tapped her on the shoulder.

"Okay," he said, "you seem to know a lot more about this than I do. I don't know who to talk to or what questions to ask. Where do I start?"

"You can start by identifying your passions," she replied.

James grinned in what he imagined was a worldly and sophisticated way.

"That's not what I mean," said Letitia. "This is serious stuff. Aren't there things you really love to do? What could you do all day without getting bored or tired?"

"Well, last summer I taught my little brother and his friends how to play baseball and I really enjoyed that. I was in the school play and I guess I got kind of choked up when the audience gave us a standing ovation. I saw the movie **Top Gun** 14 times."

"That's a start," said Letitia. "What kinds of occupations does that list suggest? Do you want to be a teacher or a coach? Do you want to take acting lessons? Maybe you'd like being an Air Force or Navy pilot. Talk to some of the people here tonight about those possibilities. But you need to give your list more thought. Keep adding to it. See where it takes you. You want to be sure that, whatever you end up doing, you'll be able to fit in activities that give you that kind of natural high."

The dictionary defines passion as a "powerful emotion; boundless enthusiasm; deep, overwhelming feeling; or avid interest." Clinical psychologist Carl Goldberg says, "Passion is the energy and enthusiasm wedded to a sense of purpose that gives life meaning and pleasure." Preparing for a career is hard work. It takes time and patience. If you choose a field that you truly love, one that excites and energizes you, you will be motivated to *do* the work, to *find* the patience. You are more likely to stick with your plan and realize your goal.

The interests, activities, or accomplishments that cause this special feeling are different for everyone. It's up to you to discover your passions. Answering the following questions should get you started. But don't stop here. Be aware of your reactions to all the ordinary and extraordinary events in your life. Keep building your list.

Identifying Your Passions

These are some of the items on Letitia's list:

Winning a debate	Chocolate	Red shoes
Dancing	The Lakers	Long walks
Texting	Social justice	*The Star-Spangled Banner*
Politics	Movies that make me cry	Writing

Complete the following statements. Don't be frustrated if you can't do it immediately. But start being aware of these feelings. As more ideas occur to you in the next weeks, turn back to this page and add them to your lists. You will continue to discover new passions throughout your life.

My heart pounds with excitement when . . .

_____

_____

I feel especially good about myself when . . .

_____

_____

I get a lump in my throat when . . .

_____

_____

I lose track of time whenever I am . . .

_____

_____

If I could be any person in history, I would be . . .

_____

_____

When I dream about my future, I see myself . . .

_____

_____

If I could change one thing about the world, it would be . . .

_____

_____

When Letitia came home, her phone was ringing. "Sorry to bother you, but I have another question."

"Yes, James, what is it?"

"I did what you suggested," he said. "I talked to the Navy recruiter about being a pilot, and I also had an interesting conversation with an actor. But I feel kind of uneasy."

"What do you mean?"

"Well, I'd like to wear a uniform and get a bunch of medals and ride in parades and stuff, but being a fighter pilot is, like . . . dangerous, you know? And it would be fun to get fan letters and have my picture in magazines and all that. But the guy I talked to said it can take years before you even get a small part—some people never make it. And all that time, you have to take classes and go to auditions—and you still have to find some way to make money, you know? So I'm confused. Part of me would really like to do these things. But another part thinks it wouldn't be that great."

"James, I think you have a values conflict here," said Letitia.

"What do you mean by 'values?'"

"Values are the standards or guiding principles that are most important to you. It sounds to me like you are seeking recognition, but you also need security. The careers you're considering are risky. You may not feel comfortable in those roles. What you need to do now is figure out what your strongest values are, and then think about careers that are compatible. Be sure that the values are yours, though. Don't just try to please others. If you aren't really committed to your goal, you won't be able to take the necessary risks or feel good about what you are doing while you're in school or just starting out. This is something you really need to think through on your own, James."

30

WORK VALUES SURVEY

What are *your* values? Is having plenty of time to spend with friends and family important to you? Or would you rather be off on some kind of adventure? Do you want to help other people? Do you want to exercise power? The following exercise should give some indication of what you value most. For each statement below, check the column that comes closest to matching your feelings.

	Very True	Some-Times True	Not Sure	Not True
1. I'd rather donate to a good cause than join a prestigious club.				
2. I'd rather have good friends than a lot of money.				
3. I'd rather have my savings in a bank account than in the stock market.				
4. I'm too adventurous to be tied down by a family.				
5. I'd like a job where I set my own hours.				
6. I enjoy books and movies where the moral to the story is not obvious.				
7. I'd rather be a scholar than a politician.				
8. I would not want to work while my children are young.				
9. I would rather write a fictional story than a research paper.				
10. When I lend money to a friend, I don't worry about being paid back.				
11. I'd rather be famous than wealthy.				
12. I would rather associate with influential people than intellectual people.				
13. Teachers should be paid as much as business executives.				
14. I'd rather go to an art museum than a sporting event.				
15. I will contribute to my retirement account before I buy extras.				
16. I prefer jobs where the duties are varied and challenging.				
17. I prefer jobs where the duties are consistent and goals are clear.				
18. I feel a person's salary indicates how much he or she is valued on the job.				
19. I would not want a high-powered job because it could strain my marriage.				
20. It is important to me that my surroundings are attractive.				
21. My reputation is worth more to me than all the money in the world.				
22. I'd rather visit a place than read about it.				
23. I'd rather know something than be *known for* something.				
24. I'd rather have a secure job than a powerful one.				
25. I'd like to be my own boss.				
26. I believe a percentage of my income should be used to help others.				
27. I would turn down a promotion if it meant I had to travel away from my family too much.				

	Very True	Some- Times True	Not Sure	Not True
28. "Money talks."				
29. I would take a cut in salary if I were offered a position in the President's Cabinet.				
30. I'd rather own a special work of art than a fancy car.				
31. I'd rather have time than money.				
32. I will always stop to watch a beautiful sunset.				
33. If my brother committed a crime, I would turn him in.				
34. I don't like to do things the same way all the time.				
35. My friendships are more precious to me than possessions.				
36. The fact that most careers that "help others" make lower wages would not stop me from entering these lines of work.				
37. It is important that I get recognition for what I do.				
38. I'd rather *work* for an exciting company than *run* a dull one.				
39. I would like to run for office in my community.				
40. I'd rather work for someone else than have my own business.				
41. The first thing I would consider when deciding on a career is how much it pays.				
42. I always take time to be a good friend.				
43. The mundane work of feeding the hungry or caring for the sick would not bother me.				
44. I don't like my decisions questioned.				
45. I'd rather have a job with a high income than one with a lot of security.				
46. It is important for me to understand how things work.				
47. I like to organize the activities of my friends and family.				
48. If I were famous, I would enjoy signing autographs.				
49. I'd rather have a secure job than an exciting one.				
50. Owning nice things is important to me.				
51. I like to do things my own way.				
52. I feel good when I volunteer my time to make my community a better place.				
53. I would never testify in court against someone in my family.				
54. It is important to me that my home is beautiful.				
55. I like to be in charge.				
56. I would rather work together with other people than alone.				
57. Books and reading are important to me.				
58. I would stand up for my beliefs even if I were punished for it.				
59. I like to solve problems.				
60. I expect to be consulted when a group I am in is making a decision.				
61. If I believed strongly in a "cause," I would make it my first priority.				
62. I have expensive tastes.				
63. If a member of my family committed a crime, I would turn him or her in to the appropriate authorities.				
64. I don't like my friends to be too dependent on me.				
65. I'd rather be married than single.				

	Very True	Some-Times True	Not Sure	Not True
66. I like to make things.				
67. My appearance is important to me.				
68. I'd love to travel around the world alone.				
69. I am sensitive to colors that clash.				
70. Someday I'd like to own my own business.				
71. I'd rather be a leader than a follower.				
72. I'd rather follow someone else.				
73. I like to learn something new everyday.				
74. I would never marry someone who had less money than I do.				
75. It is important that my mate is good looking.				
76. I would borrow money to go on a vacation.				
77. Charity begins at home.				
78. With enough money, I could be happy.				
79. I think it would be exciting to be famous.				
80. I value my privacy…I wouldn't want to be famous.				
81. I believe I should be home every night with my family and not out with friends.				
82. "Don't rock the boat."				
83. I would not take a job that I felt was unethical, no matter how much money it paid.				
84. I enjoy people who do things differently.				
85. I will go out of my way to help a stranger.				
86. I would like to have a building or street named after me.				
87. I would not lie even if telling the truth might hurt a friend's reputation.				
88. I'd rather live in a cabin in the wilderness than a beautiful home.				
89. I like to look at problems from many different angles.				
90. It is important to me to be an influential person.				
91. I'd like to be known as being one of the best in my field.				
92. I like to try new things.				
93. I will not change my views just because they're unpopular.				
94. I think you should question "rules" if they don't make sense to you.				
95. I wouldn't want to travel alone.				
96. If asked, I would serve Thanksgiving dinner to the homeless and miss my family's celebration.				
97. I always stand up for what I believe in.				
98. I wouldn't like doing the same task all day long.				
99. I like to be called in an emergency.				
100. My family will be more important to me than my career.				
101. Trophies and awards are important to me.				
102. I like to help friends with their problems.				
103. My title at work is very important to me.				
104. It is important to share my life with someone.				

Now, assign a numerical value to each of your answers. Statements in the "very true" column are worth 9 points. Those you marked "sometimes true" get 6 points. Allow 3 points for each "not sure," and zero points for every "not true" answer.

In the columns on this page and the next, write the numerical value of your response next to the statement number. For example, if you answered "very true" to the first statement, you would write a 9 on the line next to the number 1. When you have entered a number on each line, go back and total the columns under each heading.

ANSWERS

ADVENTURE	FAMILY	POWER	RECOGNITION
4. _____	8. _____	12. _____	11. _____
16. _____	19. _____	29. _____	37. _____
22. _____	27. _____	39. _____	48. _____
38. _____	53. _____	47. _____	79. _____
68. _____	65. _____	55. _____	86. _____
76. _____	77. _____	60. _____	91. _____
88. _____	81. _____	71. _____	101. _____
92. _____	100. _____	90. _____	103. _____
Total _____	Total _____	Total _____	Total _____

PERSONAL INTEGRITY & MORAL COURAGE	MONEY	SECURITY	CREATIVITY
21. _____	18. _____	3. _____	6. _____
33. _____	28. _____	15. _____	9. _____
44. _____	41. _____	17. _____	34. _____
58. _____	45. _____	24. _____	59. _____
63. _____	50. _____	40. _____	66. _____
83. _____	62. _____	49. _____	84. _____
93. _____	74. _____	72. _____	89. _____
97. _____	78. _____	82. _____	98. _____
Total _____	Total _____	Total _____	Total _____

HELPING OTHERS	KNOWLEDGE & TRUTH	FRIENDSHIP & COMPANIONSHIP
1. _____	7. _____	2. _____
26. _____	13. _____	10. _____
36. _____	23. _____	35. _____
43. _____	46. _____	42. _____
52. _____	57. _____	56. _____
85. _____	61. _____	95. _____
96. _____	73. _____	102. _____
99. _____	87. _____	104. _____
Total _____	Total _____	Total _____

BEAUTY & AESTHETICS	INDEPENDENCE & FREEDOM
14. _____	5. _____
20. _____	25. _____
30. _____	31. _____
32. _____	51. _____
54. _____	64. _____
67. _____	70. _____
69. _____	80. _____
75. _____	94. _____
Total _____	Total _____

In which category did you have the highest total? Right now, that value is most important to you. Remember, though, that values often change over time. You might want to come back to this survey every year or so when you are considering a change in your plans.

Did you have high scores in more than one category? If so, you might want to try to find a career that satisfies both or all your top values. If you value both beauty and adventure, for example, you might be happier tracking down international jewel thieves than you would be working in an art gallery or museum.

Each values category is described below:

Power

Those who value power need to prepare for leadership. Usually, that means some type of advanced education or years of experience in your trade. Most political leaders, for example, have law degrees. Business leaders quite often have a master's degree in business administration. If you value power, make sure that any job you take offers room for advancement. Or consider starting a business of your own.

Adventure

If you value adventure, you would be happiest in a career that offers some degree of variety or unpredictability. You don't necessarily have to be a spy or a soldier of fortune, but you won't want a job with too much structure or routine. Since you are probably willing to take risks, you might make a good entrepreneur.

Personal integrity and moral courage

You will be most satisfied in a career that mirrors your sense of purpose if you value personal integrity and moral purpose. Perhaps your *field* of work is less important than what you do *within* that field. For example, if you are a lawyer, you would probably be more satisfied working in legal aid than in corporate law. It is important for you to feel that your work is worthwhile to society.

Family

Those who value family are usually happiest with careers that don't call for evening or weekend work or a great deal of travel. Flexibility is helpful, as is the opportunity to work at home. A career with a salary high enough to allow you to work part-time might be attractive.

Money or wealth

Many career fields have the potential to pay very well. Make sure that the one you choose meshes with your other top values. If you also value security, for example, you might find it more satisfying to be an engineer than an entrepreneur. Remember, too, that you will probably need to spend the majority of your time working. Is there a job you would enjoy so much you wouldn't mind if it also had to be your hobby?

Knowledge and truth

If you value knowledge and truth, you might find a career that lets you pass on your knowledge—teaching, for example, or being a librarian—rewarding. Or you might prefer a job that keeps teaching *you*: doing research, investigative reporting, and the like.

Friendship and companionship

If this is your highest value, you will want to make sure that your chosen career involves working closely with others. Things to consider: Would you prefer spending your time with co-workers or clients? Do you like to see the same faces every day, or would you like to meet new people on a regular basis? Do you have a circle of friends for whom you want to reserve time?

Recognition

You may be recognized by more people if you are a TV star than if you are the best caterer in town. But, generally, you can earn recognition in just about any field if you do your job well. Choose something for which you have the necessary skills or talents, and work hard.

Independence and freedom

If this is your highest value, you may find unstructured sales—real estate or insurance, for example—rewarding. In this type of job, you can set your own hours and work without constant supervision. You might prefer to work part-time, or you might want to be self-employed. Stay away from strict schedules or jobs in which you are constantly accountable to someone else.

Security

If you value security, you will be most comfortable in a job you know will be around for a while. No new companies or risky ventures for you. You may prefer to have clearly defined duties, rather than a loosely structured job.

Beauty or aesthetics

If this is your top value, *where* you work may be almost as important a consideration as *what you do*. Your setting must be one that you find visually attractive, whether it's a garden or a cathedral. You might want your work to center on beauty, as well—perhaps you'd be happy as a designer, an architect, or a florist.

Creativity

Creative people need room to exercise their imaginations, whether they are creating a work of art, inventing a better way to display merchandise, or solving a problem in computer programming. If this is your top value, you should seek a flexible career that lets you put your ideas to work.

Helping others

If you value helping others, there are many ways for you to accomplish your goal. The service industry, in fact, is one of the fastest-growing parts of the economy. How do you want to help others? Some possibilities: you could be a paramedic, a physical therapist, a social worker, a nutritionist, a psychologist, a police officer, or a child-care worker.

Strengths and Personality

James was waiting by Letitia's locker when she arrived at school the next morning. "Hi, James!" she said. "What a surprise. What's going on?"

"Well," said James, "I thought about my values, and I think I know what they are. I really would like to be recognized, to have people know who I am. I want to keep learning, to know about things. And I'd like some adventure in my life, too—as long as it's not too risky. I mean, I'd like to go to interesting places, but I'd rather not have people shooting at me on a regular basis, if you know what I mean. But what now? Values aren't jobs. I don't think anyone is going to hire me to be a well-known person."

"Probably not," Letitia agreed. "I guess the next step is to think about your passions and values and how they relate to your personality. How do you like to work? What are your strong points? How do you feel about this? How do you feel about that? Stuff like that."

"Okay," said James. "What do you think my strengths are?"

"Well, you're curious. You're not a bit shy. And you certainly are persistent! I'm late for class. Why don't you get some opinions from your other friends?"

Everyone has his or her own way of thinking, feeling, and acting. We are all unique. Our individual characteristics develop early in childhood and usually continue in a somewhat consistent manner throughout life.

In the four columns below, you will find a list of personality traits. Circle the 10 traits you feel best describe you.

a.	b.	c.	d.
forthright	enthusiastic	steady	analytical
adventurous	expressive	amiable	controlling
forceful	influencing	predictable	perfectionist
sharp	emotional	supportive	systematic
decisive	inventive	loyal	conventional
risk taker	spontaneous	methodical	respectful
demanding	trusting	team player	meticulous
authoritative	outgoing	calm	well-disciplined
direct	unselfish	thorough	diplomatic
curious	self-assured	dependable	precise
competitive	charming	self-composed	sensitive
self-sufficient	inspiring	possessive	accurate

Now total the number circled in each column.

_____   _____   _____   _____
Total from column a   Total from column b   Total from column c   Total from column d

People have a better chance of feeling successful when they know their own work style—including their strengths and their weaknesses. Understanding the way you are likely to behave on the job will greatly enhance your ability to choose a satisfying career and lifestyle.

The ancient Greek physician Hippocrates believed people exhibited four different behavioral styles. Today many career and profile tests also use four categories to distinguish types of behavior.

Complete the following self-evaluation quiz. Circle the letter under each situation that best reflects how you would be likely to act, feel, or think.

1. Your favorite projects are ones that are
   a. likely to have favorable results.
   b. enjoyable to take part in.
   c. clearly explained.
   d. detail oriented.

2. You are on the community hospital's fund-raising committee. You would be happiest
   a. chairing the committee.
   b. publicizing the event and selling tickets.
   c. decorating the hall.
   d. keeping track of the monies collected.

3. When doing a task, you
   a. complete it in the shortest time possible.
   b. allow interruptions to take phone calls from friends.
   c. are willing to take time to help another student with their assignment.
   d. take time to check all your work for accuracy and thoroughness.

4. When faced with a stressful situation, you
   a. take charge and sometimes override the decisions of others.
   b. confront and may act in an impulsive fashion.
   c. become submissive and allow others to make your decisions.
   d. resist change and withdraw from the situation.

5. When getting dressed in the morning, you
   a. know exactly what you want to wear without giving it much thought.
   b. try on three things before deciding which is best.
   c. put on the clothes you laid out the night before.
   d. have no problem coordinating outfits because everything in your closet is in color sequence.

6. Your family is moving across the country to a lovely new home. You feel
   a. excited.
   b. curious.
   c. cautious.
   d. worried.

7. When you ask someone a question about a problem, you like an answer that
   a. is direct and to the point.
   b. includes stimulating ideas on various ways the problem could be solved.
   c. outlines the process for solving the problem.
   d. includes data and background on how the solution was reached.

8. When solving a problem, you are
   a. decisive.
   b. spontaneous.
   c. considered.
   d. deliberate.

9. When going shopping for clothes, you
   a. will not need a list. If you forget something, you'll just get it later.
   b. buy whatever catches your eye. You don't worry how different outfits go together.
   c. have a list and visit every store in town before finalizing your purchases.
   d. know exactly what you want and have searched the mall web site for sales.

Information on personality styles is adapted from the widely-used DiSC™ Dimensions of Behavior model and the *Personal Profile System*® assessment instrument, ™ copyright 1972, Carlson Learning Company. Used with permission of Carlson Learning Company, Minneapolis, Minnesota.

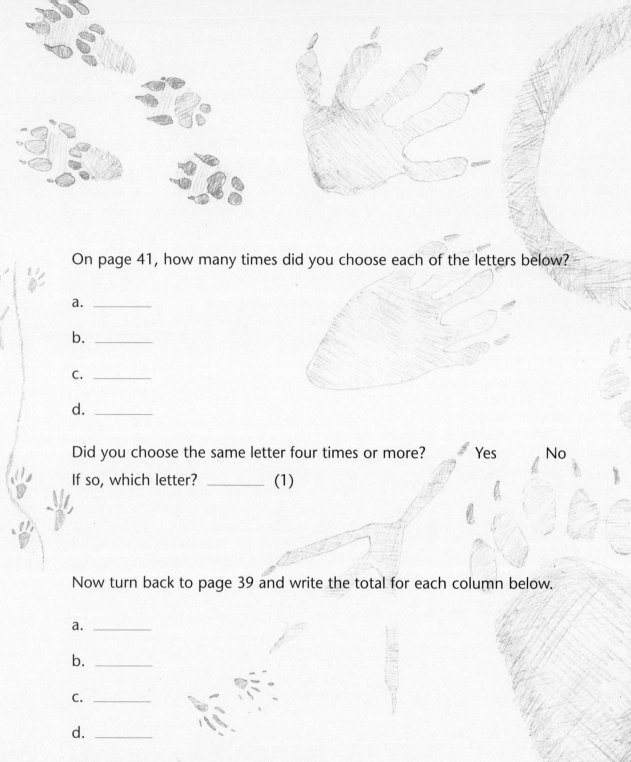

On page 41, how many times did you choose each of the letters below?

a. _____

b. _____

c. _____

d. _____

Did you choose the same letter four times or more?   Yes   No

If so, which letter? _____ (1)

Now turn back to page 39 and write the total for each column below.

a. _____

b. _____

c. _____

d. _____

Which column has the highest total? _____ (2)

Does the letter with the highest total on page 39 (line 2) match the predominant letter from the self-evaluation quiz on page 41 (line 1)?

If so, you can start identifying your work behavior style.

The four styles are as follows:

a. Dominance

People with this behavioral style like to be in control of the work environment. They are decisive and focus on accomplishing goals. They work quickly and efficiently and like tasks that are challenging. They are usually happiest in leadership positions, such as manager, store owner, entrepreneur, school principal, contractor, office manager, and so on.

b. Influencing

These people's strength lies in their ability to influence others. They are good communicators and enjoy the relationships that they develop at work. Very personable, they want recognition and a stimulating work environment. They work best in a flexible setting. They are usually happiest in people-oriented jobs such as sales, marketing, teaching, counseling, coaching, customer service, and the like.

c. Steadiness

People in this category like tasks that have well-defined procedures. Known for their steadiness and follow-through, they excel at jobs calling for specialized skills. Maintaining relationships is a high priority for them, and their home life is important. Their decisions are considered, so they are often slower to accept change. They are usually happiest in specialized positions such as word processor, mechanic, assembly line worker, repairperson, lab technician, or scientist.

d. Compliance

This category of people is responsible for quality control. They are detail people who work from a prescribed set of rules and regulations. They enjoy systematic approaches to problems and strive for accuracy. They are very precise and are well prepared. They are happiest in "watch dog" jobs: working as accountants, law enforcement officials, editors, quality control managers, building inspectors, or zoning officials.

What you have worked through is a simplified approach to analyzing your work behavior style. Very few people exhibit only one of the four profile types. There are many different combinations. The intention of this exercise is to expose you to the concept and make you aware of the possibilities available to analyze your behavior patterns. As you become more serious about choosing your career path, you will probably want to take one of the more extensive, sophisticated tests available. Many corporations use these tests in helping employees evaluate how they best work and relate to others. If you have this knowledge now it should be helpful in your career planning search. We recommend the *Personal Profile System®* from Inscape Publishing.

Information on personality styles is adapted from the widely-used DiSC™ Dimensions of Behavior model and the *Personal Profile System®* assessment instrument, ™ copyright 1972, Carlson Learning Company. Used with permission of Carlson Learning Company, Minneapolis, Minnesota.

Your Strengths

Other things to consider in choosing an appropriate career are the strong points in your personality. Are you known to be friendly? Independent? Creative? Once again, there are no "good" or "bad" traits. It's just a matter of choosing a career that's compatible and takes advantage of your strengths. For example, a friendly, outgoing person is likely to do better at and feel more satisfied with a job that provides an opportunity to make use of these social skills.

What are your strengths? It may be hard for you to list them, so get some help. One of the best ways to identify your strengths is to ask people who know you well. We all tend to be humble about such things, so your friends' and family's opinions may be more complete than your own. Ask at least six people what they feel your strengths are. It may be easiest to do this in a small group. At lunch today, why not spend time discussing personality strengths with your friends?

Turn to page 39 for a list of terms that might apply. Some other strengths might be:

adaptable, ambitious, assertive, caring, charismatic, charitable, clever, cooperative, courageous, creative, dependable, empathetic, energetic, enterprising, friendly, gracious, gentle, handy, hardworking, humorous, independent, innovative, inventive, knowledgeable, nonconformist, nurturing, open-minded, persevering, protective, realistic, reliable, resourceful, sensitive, tactful, trustworthy, unusual, versatile, well-read, willing, etc.

_____

_____

_____

_____

_____

Now complete the chart below. Choose ten of the personal strengths you have identified and list them in the first column. Then, in the second column, describe a situation or personal experience where you used these strengths or where they might be helpful.

I AM: I HAVE USED THIS STRENGTH TO:

1. _____ | _____

2. _____ | _____

3. _____ | _____

4. _____ | _____

5. _____ | _____

6. _____ | _____

7. _____ | _____

8. _____ | _____

9. _____ | _____

10. _____ | _____

Skills and Aptitudes

Letitia was ready for James when she found him back at her locker that afternoon. She took a sign she'd made in art class from her purse and taped it to her locker door. "The Career Counselor Is In," it said. "Reasonable Advice at Reasonable Rates."

"Very funny," James said. "But you're the one who got me thinking about all this stuff. Who else am I going to ask?"

"Well, there is the counseling office and the career center in the library, but I'm here right now. What can I do to help you?"

"I was just thinking. So far, we've talked about the kind of person I am, and the things I like to do. But aren't we overlooking something? Like what I'm able to do?"

"Oh, you mean your skills and aptitudes. Sure, they're important. At our age, of course, we've only begun to develop the skills we'll eventually need. But it's still a good idea to consider the things we can do now—especially the things we most enjoy."

"So where do I start?"

"Well, James, one way I've heard about is to list some of the accomplishments you're most proud of. You said you felt good about being in the play and teaching those kids how to play baseball. Take those experiences apart and think of the various skills you needed to succeed."

Though everyone has skills and aptitudes, many people are not good at recognizing them. Part of the reason for that is modesty—it seems boastful to announce that you are a terrific cook or a great musician. However, there is also an element of truly not thinking about all the skills involved in planning a party or writing a paper. James's appearance in the school play, for example, required many different skills: he had to *read* the play, *interpret* his part, *memorize* his lines, *cooperate* with others in the play, *project* his voice, and *perform* in front of hundreds of people. And many of these skills are transferable, which means that James can apply them in other situations. James has to *read* and *interpret* the reading assignments in his English class. He also has to *memorize* lyrics and *project* his voice when he *performs* with the show choir.

Since you develop skills by performing them over and over again, they are likely to be things you enjoy doing. That makes recognizing them doubly important when you plan your career: skills are things you not only *can* do, but *enjoy* doing.

An aptitude, on the other hand, is something for which you have a natural talent or something that comes easily to you. If you can sketch an accurate portrait or landscape without much effort, you can be said to have an aptitude for art. If people say you are a "natural athlete," you probably have an aptitude for sports. You may not enjoy all the subjects or activities for which you have an aptitude, but you probably will. People tend to enjoy those things that they do well.

As Letitia reminded James, you will continue to acquire skills throughout your life. In addition, some people develop skills and recognize their aptitudes later than others. So don't be discouraged if your list seems short right now. The fact that you have never built a house doesn't mean that you should give up your dream of being a carpenter.

Name That Skill

Use the following exercise to begin a list of specific skills you've mastered. Write three accomplishments that gave you the most satisfaction, or that you're most proud of, on the lines below. Then, in the middle column, list the skills you used in that enterprise. If you have a hard time identifying these skills, describe the experience to friends or family members and ask them to help you. (You'll complete the last column next.)

Accomplishment	Skills Required	Skills Category*
1.		
2.		
3.		

Do you see any pattern in the kinds of skills you used? Did they involve physical strength or coordination? Numbers or equations? Reasoning? Dealing with people?

* Basic Skills – Social Skills – Complex Problem Solving Skills – Technical Skills – Systems Skills – Resource Management Skills

Skills Identification

Each occupation requires a unique set of skills. Looking for common skill sets is one way of classifying jobs. Below are six broad **skill categories** used to group occupations on O*NET Online. Designed to group occupations that use the 35 general skills listed within these skill categories, you'll want to visit O*NET Online when you begin your research process in chapter six.

For now, review the list below and place a check mark next to each general skill that you feel competent in and an "X" next to those you want acquire in the future. Note: You're not required to select from more than one category of skills.

Basic Skills
☐ Reading Comprehension
☐ Active Listening
☐ Writing
☐ Speaking
☐ Mathematics
☐ Science
☐ Critical Thinking
☐ Active Learning
☐ Learning Strategies
☐ Monitoring

Social Skills
☐ Social Perceptiveness
☐ Coordination
☐ Persuasion
☐ Negotiation
☐ Instructing
☐ Service Orientation

Complex Problem Solving Skills
☐ Complex Problem Solving

Technical Skills
☐ Operations Analysis
☐ Technology Design
☐ Equipment Selection
☐ Installation
☐ Programming
☐ Operation Monitoring
☐ Operation and Control
☐ Equipment Maintenance
☐ Troubleshooting
☐ Repairing
☐ Quality Control Analysis

Systems Skills
☐ Judgment and Decision Making
☐ Systems Analysis
☐ Systems Evaluation

Resource Management Skills
☐ Time Management
☐ Management of Financial Resources
☐ Management of Material Resources
☐ Management of Personnel Resources

Within each of the skills listed above are more specific skills. For instance, your "repairing" skills may relate to computers or lawn movers or jet engines. Review your skills on page 47 and, in the far right column on that page, indicate which of the six skills categories relates to each one. Do you have a preference for any one skills category? If so, which one?

_____

Below list specific skills, expertise, or talents you currently have that are not listed on page 47.

_____   _____   _____

_____   _____   _____

_____   _____   _____

Can you think of skills you would like to learn but have not yet mastered? Expand the list above and be more specific. For instance, would you like to learn web design or contract negotiation, dog grooming or sales techniques?

_____   _____   _____

_____   _____   _____

_____   _____   _____

Roles, Occupations, and Vocations

The final ring on your chart asks you to list the roles, occupations, and vocations you now hold. These are very much a part of who you are, but they will change repeatedly as you get older. Today you may be someone's grandchild, for example. Some years down the road, you may be someone's *grandparent*. You will have other roles in between.

The difference between roles and occupations or vocations is simple. A role is what you are (son, daughter, sister, brother, friend, and so on). It requires no specific actions on your part. (It might be nice if you spent an hour playing video games with your little brother every night, but you will still be his brother or sister if you don't.) An occupation or vocation relates to what you do. It is something you spend time on. Occupations are paid employment. You may also be paid for your vocations, but not necessarily. A vocation is more like a special skill, something you are particularly suited to do. Right now, you are probably a student. You may have other vocations or an occupation as well (waiter or waitress, clerk, cashier, computer wizard, basketball player, musician, artist, and so on). These are more easily changed or taken away. If you don't show up for practice, you may not be a basketball player for long.

Record your present roles and occupations or vocations below, and then transfer your responses to the chart on page 27.

The Message Center

The next time Letitia saw James, he didn't seem his enthusiastic self. "Hey, James," she said, "are you okay? How's the career plan working out?"

"Oh, I don't know," he replied. "I thought about it a lot, and I finally hit on something I think I'd really like—broadcast journalism. But who do I think I'm kidding? I could never do that."

"I don't see why not," Letitia said. "You can talk. You can read. The rest of it you'll learn in college."

"Come on, Letitia. Can you imagine me on TV? No one in my family has ever even gone to college. My mom's always told me to remember where I belong, and my dad says I'm nothing but a dreamer. I guess they're probably right. I'd never make it."

"You're right. With that attitude, you never will find a way to create a future! Are you telling me your parents' fears and negative feelings are going to determine the way you feel about yourself?"

"You don't understand."

"Don't I? My father has always assumed that my brother would go to college. But not me. I'm the pretty one, he says. All I'm expected to do is get married. Sometimes I think he's right, that I'll never get into law school. But my mom believes in me. She says I can do anything I set my mind to, within reason. And I tell myself she's right. I think it's truly reasonable for you to believe you can go to college and make your dream come true.

"I know it's hard to give up those negative messages, but you've got to believe in yourself, James."

"Do you really think I could make it in TV news?" he asked.

"James, I think if you really commit yourself and give it all you've got, your chances are very high. You have the talent. If you're willing to work diligently, with no guarantee of success, I think you can make it."

We all get messages about who we are and what we should be doing from the important people in our lives. Family, teachers, friends—all let us know in various ways what they think. Some messages are hard to miss. If your father added your name to the sign on the family business the day you were born, there's not much doubt where he thinks your future lies. More subtly, a parent who always steps in to help you finish your homework, or rewashes the floor as soon as you put your mop away, gives the message that you are not competent to do something yourself.

Messages like these are limiting and destructive. They can make you feel that you have few choices in life, or that you just don't measure up. Other messages—like Letitia's to James, or her mother's to Letitia—are positive and empowering. They can build your confidence and help you achieve your dreams.

It's important to recognize the messages you get from your significant others because they are powerful and pervasive. They are like tapes playing over and over in the back of your mind, and they are difficult to erase.

Negative or limiting messages may come back to haunt you throughout your life, especially in certain situations. For example, if you've been given the message that you are too shy to have fun at parties, a little voice will crop up every time you get an invitation: "I'm no good at parties. I don't want to go." If you are aware of this fact, however, you can learn to dismiss the message and act more freely: "Thank you for sharing that, but I think I will go to the party and have a good time."

What messages have you received? For the following exercise, write what you think the significant people in your life would tell you about your future. Imagine them leaving their message on your voicemail.

Hello, you have reached _____'s message center. What would you like to tell me about my future? BEEP!

Mother's message: _____

_____

Father's message: _____

_____

Teacher's message: _____

_____

Other significant adult's message (coach, mentor, boss, relative): _____

_____

_____

Best friend's message: _____

_____

Girlfriend or boyfriend's message: _____

_____

Some of the strongest messages we receive come from society. Sex, age, race, nationality, religion, physical appearance, physical or intellectual abilities, financial status, social class—any of these can be the basis for taunts and jeers or praise and affection, great expectations or limited hope. What messages has society given you?

Society's message:

_____

_____

_____

Now go back and circle the messages that are limiting or negative. How much importance should you place on other people's opinions of you and their plans for your life? Should you have to live up to other people's goals and ideals? Whose life is it, anyway?

Positive Messages to Yourself

What positive messages can you give yourself about your future? Write them below. Recite them to yourself often, or read them into a digital voice recorder and play them again and again while you're relaxing.

1. _____

_____

2. _____

_____

3. _____

_____

4. _____

_____

5. _____

_____

When you have completed all the exercises in this chapter, go back to page 27 and add what you've learned about yourself to the diagram there.

Who you are, of course, cannot be summed up by a bunch of words on a chart. You are a complex and constantly changing person, an individual unlike any other who's ever existed. The exercises in this chapter should, however, provide some insights that can help you make sound decisions for your future. The next step is deciding what you want.

There is only one success — to be able to
spend your life in your own way.
— Christopher Morley

Happiness is not a state to arrive at, but
a manner of traveling.
— Margaret Lee Runbeck

CHAPTER THREE

Lifestyles of the Satisfied and Happy

Keeping your balance and perspective

Section Two:
WHAT DO I WANT?

Deciding what you want from life is not an easy task. What you want today is probably quite different from what you wanted 10 years ago. And, in another 10 years, your wants may well have changed again. That's to be expected. What you want usually depends on who you think you are at the time. As you change, so do your needs and desires.

In general, though, most people want happiness, peace, and life satisfaction. However, the things that will *give* them these feelings vary greatly. Contrary to popular opinion, money and outward signs of success don't have much to do with life satisfaction. That comes from *inside,* from your own unique achievements and sense of self.

Again, though, these will change. Perhaps this section of the book should be titled "What Do I Want *Now*?" This is something you need to re-evaluate on a regular basis. The processes you'll learn in the following chapters should help.

To paraphrase Mick Jagger, "You can't get what you want 'til you get what you need." Fortunately for us, someone has already determined the things we all need in order to be fully satisfied—and the order in which we must have them. The psychologist Abraham Maslow developed what has come to be called the Maslow Triangle. It graphically illustrates this hierarchy of human needs.

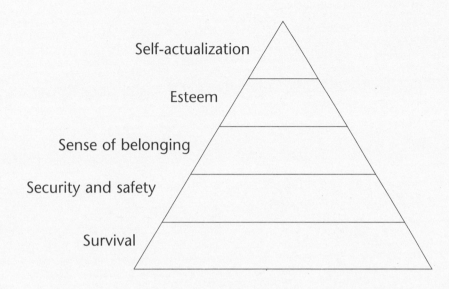

It's important to become familiar with this diagram. Deciding what you want from life is difficult. If you can place yourself on a particular level of the triangle, you will have a better understanding of what you need to do next.

Think of the triangle as a ladder, with the bottom rung at the triangle's base. You cannot jump over a rung or two. You must take each step in order if you want to reach the top. (It's quite possible to slip down the rungs, but let's not get ahead of ourselves.) Let's look at the triangle.

According to Dr. Maslow, our first need is simply to **survive**. We must have food, water, clothing, and shelter. Until we have these basic necessities, we cannot move on to consider our next need, which is for **safety and security**. The first two rungs deal only with physical and emotional survival—not a very satisfying way to live for most people.

When you hit the third level of the triangle, your need for other people becomes apparent. Some people are more dependent on relationships than others, but we all need to feel connected to other human beings. We all need to have a **sense of belonging**.

As we near the top of the triangle, we find that we have a need for **esteem**. We want other people to feel that we are worthy of respect. We also want to respect ourselves. At this point, we become capable of thinking about what we want, rather than simply about what we need.

Finally, at the peak of the triangle is the need for what Maslow calls **"self-actualization."** Self-actualized people are those who have done what they set out to accomplish, who have reached their goals. Not many people reach this point (only about 10 percent), and not everyone who gets there stays there. Some people continue to set new goals every time they reach their old ones.

Other people can quickly slide back to a lower rung. For example, people who lose their jobs or their health may find themselves back seeking survival and safety. Until they re-achieve these needs, they cannot approach—or probably even give much thought to—their higher needs.

As you think about your current place in the hierarchy of needs, it is important to remember that achieving life satisfaction is a *process*. It can only be accomplished one step at a time.

So be patient with yourself. It may be years before you can say exactly what you want from life. Even then, you may change your mind. The world is full of middle-aged people who are still trying to decide what they want to be when they grow up.

The process of thinking about your identity and your future can be rewarding in itself. It can get you headed in the right direction. It can help you realize that you have some control over your life.

Where Are You Now?

Answer the following questions to determine your present location on the Maslow Triangle. If you answer yes to the questions in each section, color in the corresponding section on the triangle below.

SURVIVAL

Do you have enough food and water to survive?	Yes	No
Do you have a place to live?	Yes	No
Do you have enough clothes to keep you warm?	Yes	No

SECURITY AND SAFETY

Do you feel safe?	Yes	No
Do you feel secure?	Yes	No

SENSE OF BELONGING

Do you feel you belong somewhere?	Yes	No
Do you feel loved?	Yes	No

SELF-ESTEEM

Do you feel good about yourself?	Yes	No
Do you feel worthwhile or valuable as a human being?	Yes	No

SELF-ACTUALIZATION

Do you feel accomplished?	Yes	No
Do you feel mature?	Yes	No
Do you trust your judgment?	Yes	No
Do you feel in control of your life?	Yes	No

Self-actualization

Esteem

Sense of belonging

Security and safety

Survival

How Do You Want to be Remembered?

Walter Johnson always seemed to be three steps ahead of everyone else. When other children his age were learning to crawl, Walter was learning to in-line skate. "A much more efficient means of transportation," he explained to his mother.

At five, Walter was memorizing Homer's **Odyssey**—in Greek. "Such a musical language," he said. Few people were surprised when Walter graduated at the top of his college class at age 14.

But even his mother was shocked to find 16-year-old Walter carving his own tombstone in the family basement. "What are you doing?" she exclaimed. "Are you sick? What's going on? You have to tell me!"

"I'm fine, Mom," he said. "No sense putting this off until the last minute. Besides, I have a use for it now. I need it to show me how to live."

"What do you mean?" she asked.

"I've carved it right here—what I want to be remembered for. For now, it will be my guide. It will help me make decisions and make the best use of my time."

He held up the stone. WALTER JOHNSON, it said. HE GAVE IT HIS BEST SHOT.

It may seem odd, but Walter's idea is a good one. One of the best ways to determine what you really want out of life is to think about how you want to be remembered after death. Caught up in the demands of day-to-day living, we often lose track of our fondest dreams, our mission in life, our legacy.

We all want to be recognized or acknowledged for some action, way of being, or accomplishment. This is a basic human need. Taking the time now to think about the contribution you would like to make in your lifetime will help give your life direction.

How would you like to be remembered? Do any of these epitaphs strike a chord?

JACK LITTLE: BEST COOK IN CHICAGO

SARITA PATEL: EVERYBODY LOVED HER

FARID MANSOUR: A NEW CAR EVERY YEAR

BERTA SANTINI: CRUSADER FOR JUSTICE

MAURICIO PEREZ: HE MADE PEOPLE LAUGH

AN NGUYEN: FIRST WOMAN PRESIDENT OF THE UNITED STATES

SAMUEL STEVENS: TEACHER OF THE YEAR

LUCY BARTON: PROUD OWNER OF 139 PAIRS OF SHOES

CONNIE FITZPATRICK: WORLD TRAVELER

LEWIS JONES: PEACEMAKER

ROBERTA ZIMMER: SUPERSTAR

HAROLD CLAUSSEN: FAMILY MAN

MARGARET GONZALES: PHILANTHROPIST

LEE CHUNG: POET

In the space below, write your own epitaph. How do you want to be remembered? At the end of your life, what would you have to have done in order to be thought of that way? You don't have to limit your answer to a single line, but keep it brief.

Try not to get hung up on external forms of success, such as making a million dollars. You are more likely to be remembered—and to feel good about yourself—because of what you do with the money. If you must have that million, consider how you would use it. Would you set up a scholarship fund? Build a wing of a hospital? Assure the future security of your family? Save the whales? Retire and become a community volunteer?

Consider your personal heroes. These might be world figures like Nelson Mandela or Mohandas Gandhi, or they might be known only to a few, such as the coach who made you believe in yourself or the stutterer who landed the lead in the class play. What do these people tell you about your values?

Think about your passions and your dreams as well. And remember that, unlike Walter's, *your* mission is not carved in stone. It may change as you develop new beliefs, dreams, and goals.

_____ : _____
Your Name

_____

_____

Your Lifestyle

As you may be beginning to see, your career choice will affect more than the 40 hours a week you'll spend on the job. A job title often suggests a whole way of life. Rock star, scientist, farmer, carpenter—when we think of people in these occupations, we immediately visualize what they wear, where they live, who their friends are, perhaps even the person they voted for in the last election. (We may be *wrong,* mind you. But, in general, you won't find too many farmers in Manhattan. And most scientists are not close personal friends of Eric Clapton.) In short, your career will help define your lifestyle.

What do we mean when we talk about lifestyle? Until recently, the word didn't even appear in the dictionary. But sociologists and psychologists have come to realize that the way people live, the way they think and feel, what's important to them, and how they spend their time, money, and energy help explain not only individual lives, but how and why our society works the way it does. The term *lifestyle* is a composite of your income and education, your attitudes, your political and spiritual beliefs, where you choose to live, how you earn and spend your money, what is most important to you—even how secure and happy you are likely to be.

Before you begin researching possible careers, it is important to try to determine what type of lifestyle you want. Your career choice will have a great impact on the type of lifestyle you will lead.

COMPONENTS OF LIFESTYLE

Lifestyle has many components. We've listed some below. Think about your ideal future life and complete this questionnaire as best you can.

RELATIONSHIPS

Do you want to be married? _____ Have children? _____ If so, how many? _____

What kinds of people would you like to be your friends? _____

_____

How much time (hours per week) will you want to spend with your family? Your friends?

_____

WORK

How much time do you want to spend at your chosen profession? Less than 20 hours per week? 20–40 hours per week? 40–50 hours? As long as it takes?

_____

What is your mission in life? What sort of commitment do you want or need to make to some larger goal?

_____

PERSONAL

How much time each week would you like to spend on:

Recreation _____ Individual pursuits _____ Contemplation and relaxation _____

How much flexibility do you want in your life? _____

What will be the "pace" of your life? Are you a high-energy person who always needs to have many projects at once, or are you a person who likes to tackle one thing at a time?

_____

How will you meet your spiritual needs? _____

MATERIAL ITEMS

Where do you want to live? Describe the location and housing. _____

_____

What income level would you like to reach? _____

Describe the possessions you want most. _____

_____

Happiness Is a Balanced Lifestyle

Emma is a stockbroker who is totally dedicated to her work. She seldom gets home before 10 at night, and is back at her desk by 7:00 A.M. She devotes her weekends to reading annual reports and books and articles dealing with her job. She hasn't taken a vacation in five years and has no close friends or outside interests.

Isaac is a police officer in a small town. He and his wife have two children. He volunteers at a homeless shelter two nights a week and coaches his daughters' softball team. In order to save money, Isaac and his wife are renovating their house by themselves. He attends night school, working toward a degree in criminology. Issac is also a guitarist with a small band that plays for local social events. He tries to do his share of the housework and thinks it's important to spend time with his children each day. Isaac and his wife go out alone at least once a week. His parents are getting older, and he likes to see them often. He enjoys going out with his friends.

Emma and Isaac have little in common—except that both have problems balancing their lives. Emma's life is incomplete. There are times when it is necessary to center your attention on one part of your life (finishing a project at work or recuperating from an illness, for example). However, Emma may never be truly happy if she keeps up her current pattern indefinitely. She needs to look at Maslow's Triangle.

Isaac is probably already aware that his life is *too* full. Some people have enormous amounts of energy and are able to juggle a wide variety of interests, activities, and responsibilities, but there are only 24 hours in a day and everyone has to sleep *sometime.* Isaac needs to decide which activities are most important to him and which ones he can most easily give up.

The exact makeup of a balanced lifestyle will be different for everyone. Some people want to give most of their attention to their work. For others, family is most important. Some people want or need to give priority to health concerns. But, in general, an emotionally and physically healthy life will include time for the following:

Physical health: Time to sleep and eat wisely must be built into every balanced lifestyle. Healthy people need time for both exercise and relaxation. Other health needs vary.

Work: Work is a central activity and source of identity for most adults. How important is it for you? Will you work part-time? Full-time? More than 40 hours a week? Would you like to be able to take time out when you have small children?

Family/relationships: Will you marry and have children? Marry and *not* have children? Surround yourself with a group of close friends? Today, there is a wide range of acceptable ways to meet your needs for close relationships with others. Your best choice might depend on the weight you assign other parts of your life. For example, Emma would almost certainly be happier if she had good friends and a circle of acquaintances she could socialize with regularly. Whether she would be happy marrying a man with three children is questionable.

Do you want to have children? They take time and attention, especially when they are young. How would you adjust your lifestyle to accommodate them? For example, could you earn enough money working part-time? Could you work at home?

Leisure and recreation: Your balanced lifestyle should include time for hobbies, avocations, and the leisure activities that add so much to life. Will you travel? Have a garden? Follow your favorite sport or athletic team? Read or go to the movies?

Spiritual life: The dictionary defines spirit as "that which constitutes one's unseen, intangible being" or "the essential and activating principle of a person." Many people realize their spiritual needs through their religion. Others choose to "give something back" to the world by working as a volunteer or getting involved with organizations that promote conservation, peace, or human rights. Some people meet their spiritual needs privately, through meditation, reading, walking, and the like.

With all these considerations, it's easy to see how a life can get off balance!

The Modified Maslow Triangle

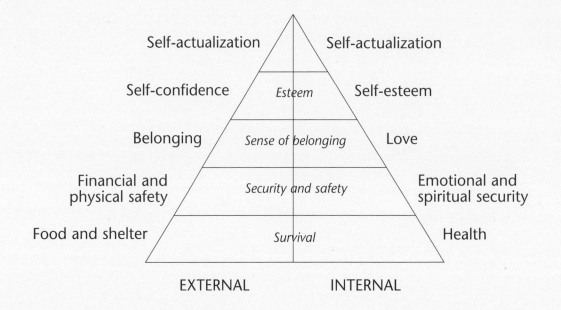

To make it easier to visualize a balanced lifestyle, we have divided Maslow's Triangle down the middle. Although the hierarchy of needs remains the same, *our* triangle differentiates professional, or external, needs (shown on the left side) from personal, or internal, needs (diagrammed on the right).

> **Our external lives** include such things as careers, the tasks we do, the possessions we accumulate, the roles we play, and the way others see us. Our social and educational systems teach us to deal almost exclusively with this side of life.

> **By internal lives**, we mean our physical and spiritual well-being, our values, and our personal relationships. This is the side of life society tends to ignore. This may account for the increased use of drugs, depression, divorce, and general discontent we are experiencing today.

If either side is given too much emphasis, our lives become unbalanced. Life satisfaction decreases. It is possible on our double triangle to achieve one level of fulfillment in career life and quite another in personal matters. The happiest people are those who engage in both aspects of life. They are less willing to sacrifice one part for the sake of the other.

But it's often a difficult balancing act. Today, especially, men and women attempting to mix career and family are having problems finding the time for all the important activities in their lives. It takes careful and creative planning to balance all of the areas of your life.

Let's go through our divided triangle, level by level. It's necessary to repeat ourselves somewhat, so please be patient.

Just as the most basic external need is for **food and shelter** (left), **good health** is the most basic personal need (right). Until we have these, we are unable to satisfy the next level of needs—**financial and physical safety** on the left side, **spiritual and emotional security** on the right side. It is impossible for most people to experience life satisfaction unless they reach these first two levels of fulfillment. Yet many people begin to make trade-offs here. They sacrifice their health in order to make more money even though, without good health, they cannot hope to enjoy their lives.

Those who feel confident of the ability to support themselves—without giving up physical or emotional health—can move on to the next level of need: **love** (on the right or personal side) and **belonging** (on the left or professional side). Although it is important to "belong," to have a circle of acquaintances and casual friends, it is also necessary to have at least one deeper relationship. This might be with a spouse, a best friend, or someone else to whom you feel particularly close and committed.

People who do not have satisfying relationships with others cannot move on to achieve **self-confidence and achievement** (on the external side) and self-esteem (an internal need). At this level, you like yourself and feel good about what you are doing. Again, we see the necessity to consider the needs on both sides of the triangle. You might feel confident of your ability to succeed by cheating, lying, or manipulating, but if success comes at the expense of your **self-esteem**, it is not likely to make you happy. Shortcuts, even when successful, carry costs that will lessen good feelings.

Once you have attained both confidence and self-esteem, you are on your way to becoming one of those rare **self-actualizers**, someone who is satisfied and happy with her or his life.

How can you tell if you are neglecting one side of your life? Besides the obvious ways—losing your health, your job, your close relationship—listen to your inner voice. Be aware of your feelings. Do you ever begin sentences with phrases such as "if only," "I wish," "I should but I can't," or "If I had the time I would?" These are clues that your life is not as satisfying as it might be. It's time to take a closer look and make some changes.

Let's see what Emma's and Isaac's diagrams might look like:

Emma has a good job and the respect of her colleagues and superiors. She thinks her work is of value, and loves what she does. Because she puts in so many hours, however, she has no time for personal relationships or private interests, and the stress of her job has placed her health in jeopardy. Emma's triangle looks like this:

Isaac, too, has a good job and the respect of his community. He feels good about working toward his degree in criminology. He loves his wife and children and has many friends. But he seems to be exhausted all the time because of all he does. And he gets down on himself because he can't always do what he's promised. Many of his projects are done haphazardly or not completed. Isaac's triangle looks like this:

Especially when you don't make conscious changes in your life, things can get off kilter over time. That's why it is important to re-evaluate your situation regularly and try to become more aware of your feelings.

When Joanie was 25, she had a financially secure job that she loved, the respect of her fellow workers, and a circle of devoted and loving friends. Shade the triangle below to represent the levels Joanie had attained in both her professional and personal life.

By the time she was 30, things had changed. Her job seemed less satisfying, though she put in many hours. The resulting stress caused health problems. Many of her friends had married and started families or moved away to take new jobs, and Joanie's social life dramatically changed. She thought she might like to have a family of her own, but she wasn't dating anyone at the moment. Shade this triangle to show how Joanie's life had changed.

69

What About Your Life?

Describe your life right now:

How is your health? Do you get enough to eat? Do you have adequate housing? Do you feel financially secure and physically safe? Do you feel emotionally secure? Are your spiritual needs being met? Do you feel you belong to a group? Do you feel loved? Do you like yourself? Do you feel confident about your abilities and who you are? Are you satisfied and happy?

Shade the triangle below to show the balance in your life right now. Do you need to make any adjustments? What could you do to make your life more satisfying?

Now interview one of your parents or another adult you know and interpret his or her responses to the above questions.

Shade the triangle below to show his or her balance.

What do you think the triangle of a homeless person living alone would look like?

Self-actualization	Self-actualization
Self-confidence	Self-esteem
Belonging	Love
Financial and physical safety	Emotional and spiritual security
Food and shelter	Health
EXTERNAL	INTERNAL

Your desired lifestyle is something to be considered when making career decisions. As you will see in the next chapter, however, any way of life you choose involves costs as well as rewards. These might relate to finances, psychological rewards or sacrifices, or the degree of commitment required.

It's good to have money and the things
money can buy, but it's good too, to
check once in a while and make sure
that you haven't lost the things that
money can't buy.
— George Horace Lorimer

I'd rather have roses on my table
than diamonds on my neck.
— Emma Goldman

CHAPTER FOUR

What Cost This Lifestyle ?

Every career choice involves sacrifices
and rewards

Visit http://www.careerchoices.com when you
see this logo:

You'll find valuable Internet resources, calculators,
and charts that will enhance your understanding
of the topics found on that page.

Section Two:
WHAT DO I WANT?

Ralph Tuttle, young business reporter for the *Daily Bugle*, was upset. His interview with Ivy Elms, the highest paid executive in the world, was not proceeding as expected. This was supposed to be Ralph's big chance. He could almost see the headlines: IVY ELMS REVEALS SECRETS FOR SUCCESS TO JUNIOR REPORTER. Instead, the famous executive was running on about things that made no sense to Ralph. Was she senile? Ralph cheered up a bit. Maybe that was another angle he could use for his story.

"Making a lot of money can be one of the most expensive things in the world," Ivy said when Ralph tuned back in to the interview. "I'm lucky I can afford this job."

"Wow," Ralph thought. "The old girl really is going off the deep end." He decided to play along with her. "Just what do you mean by that, Miss Elms?"

Ivy poured herself a glass of mineral water from the crystal decanter on her enormous rosewood desk. She removed two tablets from a sterling silver pill box, explaining, "This one's for my blood pressure, and this for my ulcer. Been taking them for years. Fortunately, I've never had any real health problems. Health is one of the first things a high-pressure job like this can cost."

Ralph's face brightened. "OH! I get it. You mean making a lot of money is expensive because of the other things you have to give up, right?"

"I knew you'd catch on sooner or later," Ivy said.

"So what else has your success cost you?"

"One of the sad things is that you never know exactly what your life might have been. No one ever knows that. So you just have to go after what seems most important. I always wanted to be a big success in business. This company has been my family, my best friend, my only hobby. I invested my life in it, you might say. I never married or had children—didn't think I could spare the time. And I often wonder if people are nice to me only because they want something they think I can give them.

"This power to affect so many lives is a big responsibility. I worry about it. What happens if I make a mistake and profits fall and I have to lay some people off? There's no one else to blame. I also worry about leaving the company in good shape. There are all those young, ambitious people out there wanting to take my job away from me. That makes me more determined, and then I work a little harder, which takes its toll on my health and my sense of humor.

"But I got what I wanted and, more or less, I'm happy with that. I live very well — beautiful homes, expensive cars, even a corporate jet. I'm known and respected all over the world. I have the pleasure of knowing that I do an important job, and that I do it better than anyone.

"Always remember, Mr. Tuttle, every job has its costs as well as its rewards. I have wealth, position, and power, but I will always wonder what it's like to have a family."

After the interview, Ralph asked himself what Ivy's story might mean for him. He thought about the way he lived and the way he'd like to live. How important was money to him, he wondered. What did he need to make his life meaningful? Ivy had set her goal early, and she stuck to her plan. She invested heavily in her career. Ralph thought about the commitment that called for and wondered if he was willing to follow through in the same way.

Nothing is ever enough when what you are looking for isn't what you really want.
— Arianna Stassinopoulos Huffington

75

Every job involves three different kinds of rewards—and sacrifices. The most obvious consideration is financial—how much money can you expect to earn at this job? Your salary will visibly affect your lifestyle. That is why it is essential to consider the cost—in dollars—of the material things you want to include in your life when making career decisions. Is it reasonable to expect that an elementary school teacher will be delivered to his classroom in a chauffeur-driven limousine?

The second consideration involves the physical, emotional, or psychological rewards and sacrifices of a given career. This concern is tied directly to your own values. What is most important to you? The idea is not to find a job that offers only rewards—as far as we can determine, no such job exists. However, one person's reward may be a sacrifice to someone else. Being a politician, for example, may offer large rewards to someone who values recognition. For someone who values privacy, though, this career would require a big sacrifice. When you look at potential careers, consider both the rewards and the sacrifices and try to find one that matches your own values closely.

The third consideration is commitment. Do you want this job or lifestyle badly enough to invest the required time, money, and energy to prepare for it? Some people decide to scale down their dreams when they find they don't have the "stick-to-itiveness" to make them come true, or if they think the sacrifices are too great. For example, one man we know who grew up believing he would be head of a major corporation abandoned that plan to work for a smaller firm. The change allows him to pursue other interests and to have more time for family and community affairs. He thinks the trade-off was worthwhile.

This chapter is designed to help you determine just how much your dream lifestyle will cost: in money, in physical and emotional health, and in commitment.

To begin, you need to consider the income you would need to support your ideal lifestyle.

Your Budget

Let's talk about the kind of lifestyle you want to have—and how much money it is likely to cost. The following exercise asks you to make choices about everything from where you'd like to live to the vacations you'd like to take. Charts are provided to show approximate costs for many choices. Better yet, the Internet is a wonderful financial resource tool. The calculators and information available online will help you customize your budget to the penny. Once you make your choices in each category, enter your monthly expense in the space provided.

Since the point of the exercise is to help you make career decisions for your future, don't base your choices on what you think is realistic for you right now. Instead, think of the way you would like to be living at some specific age. (Make it at least 29 years old.)

Choose an age and then complete this statement: Today, I am _____ years old.
In _____ years, when I am _____ years old, this is how I would like my life to look.

FAMILY PROFILE

The first choice you need to make concerns your future family. In the real world, this choice is not totally under your control; for now, dream away. Check the marital status you see for yourself at the age you've chosen, and indicate the number of children you'll have, if any. Fill in the ages of your children.

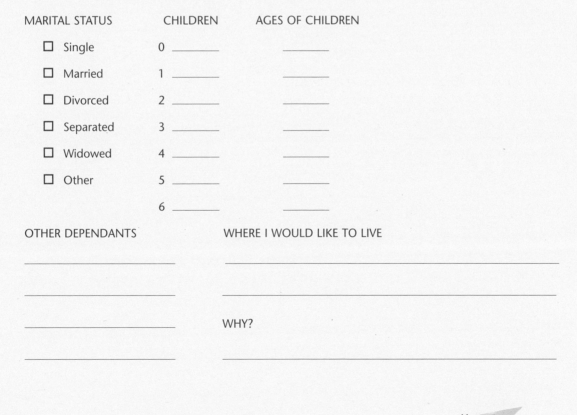

MARITAL STATUS	CHILDREN	AGES OF CHILDREN
☐ Single	0 _____	_____
☐ Married	1 _____	_____
☐ Divorced	2 _____	_____
☐ Separated	3 _____	_____
☐ Widowed	4 _____	_____
☐ Other	5 _____	_____
	6 _____	_____

OTHER DEPENDANTS

_____

_____

_____

_____

WHERE I WOULD LIKE TO LIVE

_____

_____

WHY?

_____

_____

Housing

Housing is the most expensive item on most people's budget. It is possible that your future spouse, a titled aristocrat, will inherit the family estate (tax-free, of course). But don't count on it. For the purpose of this exercise, assume that you will have to allot a portion of your income for a place to live.

Keep your own values in mind as you complete this exercise. It's *your* dreams we're interested in, not your mom's or your best friend's.

Do you want to live in:

☐ Government housing   ☐ A farm or ranch

☐ A rental apartment   ☐ A cabin

☐ A cooperative apartment   ☐ A luxury home/estate

☐ A rental house   ☐ No permanent home

☐ Your own home   ☐ Other _____

☐ A condominium

How many bedrooms? _____ Bathrooms? _____

Other distinguishing features _____

_____

Check the classified advertisement section of a newspaper or a local realtor's web site to get an idea of the sales price of homes and rental rates. The charts on the next page may help you figure your monthly costs.

Monthly payment/rent	$ _____
Monthly property taxes	$ _____
Monthly insurance	$ _____
Total utilities/phone	$ _____
Housing	$ _____ [1]

Enter at [1] on page 92, Your Budget Profile.

Here are some interesting charts for comparison.

HOME AFFORDABILITY, CITY BY CITY

City	Median Income	Average Home Price	Affordability Ratio*
Albany, NY	$75,500	$227,608	33%
Albuquerque, NM	$60,300	$355,169	17%
Bakersfield, CA	$51,900	$230,251	23%
Baton Rouge, LA	$60,600	$246,106	25%
Bridgewater, NJ	$78,300	$545,381	14%
Cleveland, OH	$64,800	$87,240	74%
Dallas, TX	$68,300	$180,228	38%
Fargo, ND	$68,100	$200,517	34%
Indianapolis, IN	$68,700	$179,298	38%
Las Vegas, NV	$65,700	$167,133	39%
Memphis, TN	$58,100	$126,617	46%
Oklahoma City, OK	$59,400	$171,095	35%
Philadelphia, PA	$78,300	$321,528	24%
Portland, OR	$71,200	$417,395	17%
Providence, RI	$72,100	$144,900	50%
Raleigh, NC	$77,700	$280,502	28%
Richmond, VA	$73,900	$241,634	31%
Saint Paul, MN	$84,000	$236,491	36%
Salt Lake City, UT	$70,000	$401,354	17%
Seattle, WA	$81,700	$688,270	12%
Topeka, KS	$61,300	$116,343	53%
Tucson, AZ	$61,500	$307,841	20%

* Affordability ratio figures calculated using information from Fannie Mae and Coldwell Banker.

Hint: The higher the affordability ratio, the easier it is to purchase a home. The annual income in Topeka purchases 53% of a typical home, while the annual income in Seattle purchases on 12% of an average-priced home.

Source: Fannie Mae, 2010-2011 HUD Area Median Income Search. (www.fanniemae.com)

Source: Coldwell Banker, Home Price Comparison Index, 2010 Domestic Survey.

RENTING VERSUS OWNING?

Location	Monthly Costs	
	Owning	Renting
New York, NY	$7,083	$3,327
San Diego, CA	$2,263	$1,278
Jacksonville, FL	$1,028	$758
Atlanta, GA	$823	$795
Indianapolis, IN	$828	$628
Cleveland, OH	$788	$696

Source: Marcus & Millichap Research Services, Federal Housing Finance Board, National Association of Realtors, Reis Inc., 2009.

PLANNING MONTHLY PAYMENTS
Monthly Payment per $1,000

Rate	15-year	30-year
4%	$7.40	$4.77
5%	$7.91	$5.37
6%	$8.44	$6.00
7%	$8.99	$6.66
8%	$9.56	$7.34
9%	$10.15	$8.05
10%	$10.75	$8.78
11%	$11.37	$9.53

Use this table to figure monthly principle-and-interest payments on 30-year and 15-year loans. For example, to find the monthly payment on a $150,000, 30-year loan at 7%, multiply $6.66 by 150. Monthly payment: $999.00.

MONTHLY MORTGAGE PAYMENTS IF INTEREST IS:
(factored at 30-year fixed rate and includes insurance and taxes)

Loan Amount	5%	7%	9%	11%	Insurance	Taxes
$40,000	$215	$266	$322	$381	$10	$32
$60,000	$322	$399	$483	$571	$15	$48
$80,000	$429	$532	$644	$762	$20	$64
$100,000	$537	$665	$805	$952	$25	$80
$120,000	$644	$798	$966	$1,143	$30	$96
$140,000	$752	$931	$1,126	$1,333	$35	$112
$175,000	$939	$1,164	$1,408	$1,667	$44	$140
$200,000	$1,074	$1,331	$1,609	$1,905	$50	$160
$300,000	$1,610	$1,996	$2,414	$2,857	$75	$240

FIRST-TIME HOMEBUYER AFFORDABILITY, 2011

Starter Home Price	10% Down Payment	Loan Amount	Effective Interest Rate	Plus PMI*	Monthly Payment	Qualifying Income
$145,000	$14,520	$130,500	4.62	4.87	$690	$33,120

Source: National Association of Realtors, 2011.
* PMI – Private Mortgage Insurance

Transportation

Before you choose the kind of transportation you'll want or need, think about where you said you'd like to live. In some cities, it's quite easy to walk or use public transportation. In some places, a vehicle is almost a necessity. Consider, too, your physical condition and your mechanical ability.

Do you want to get around by:

☐ Walking

☐ Bicycle

☐ Motorcycle

☐ Public transportation

☐ Your own car, previously owned

☐ Your own car, bought new every 7–8 years

☐ Your own car, bought new every 3–4 years

☐ Your own car, bought new every year

☐ Limousine

☐ Other _____

If you want to own your own car:

What make? _____ Model? _____ Year? _____

How many miles per month do you plan to drive? _____

Monthly car payments	$ _____
Gasoline	$ _____
Maintenance and insurance	$ _____
Public transportation	$ _____
Transportation	$ _____ [2]

Enter at [2] on page 92.

CareerChoices.com

My 10yearPlan.com

NEW CAR PRICES		
Domestic	Import	Average
$22,503	$25,874	$23,420

Source: U.S. Department of Commerce, Bureau of Economic Analysis, Gross Domestic Product Fourth Quarter 2010.

PASSENGER CAR OPERATING COSTS

	Variable Costs in Cents per Mile				Cost per 10,000 Miles			
	Gas	Maintenance	Tires	Variable Total	Variable Cost	Fixed Cost*	Total Cost	Total Cost Per Mile
Medium Sedan	$0.120	$0.044	$0.009	$0.173	$1,730	$5,841	$7,571	$0.757
4WD Sport Utility Vehicle	$0.164	$0.050	$0.010	$0.223	$2,231	$7,738	$9,969	$0.997

* Fixed Costs include annual cost of insurance, license, registration, taxes, depreciation, and finance charges.
 Source: AAA (American Automobile Association), "Your Driving Costs," 2010 Edition.

Clothing

Your clothing budget depends on your talents, your tastes, and the time you want to devote to this part of your life. Perhaps you are one of those creative types who can whip up exciting outfits from plastic bags and old neckties. Maybe you always have and always will live in blue jeans. Bargain hunters, given enough time, can produce expensive designer wardrobes at discount store prices. Others wouldn't consider buying anything at less than full price. Some people, short on time, are willing to spend whatever is necessary to get what they need in a hurry.

Think about how much money you feel would be a reasonable amount to spend each year on clothing for yourself and each member of your family. How do you prefer to come by your clothes? Do you want or need an extensive wardrobe, or will just the basics do? Don't forget to make allotments for shoes, bathing suits, and other items that may not come immediately to mind. Then answer the questions below.

For clothing, I plan to:

☐ Sew for the family

☐ Purchase thrift store or "vintage" clothing

☐ Buy from discount or outlet stores

☐ Always buy on sale

☐ Buy from department stores and boutiques

☐ Buy designer fashions

☐ Other _____

I would like to have:

☐ A minimum wardrobe

☐ A moderate-size wardrobe

☐ An extensive wardrobe

☐ What I want, when I want it

My
10yearPlan
.com

List each member of your family and his or her projected clothing budget:

Family Member   Annual Budget

_____ $ _____

_____ $ _____

_____ $ _____

_____ $ _____

_____ $ _____

_____ $ _____

Annual Family Total $ _____

Divide this figure by 12 to get your monthly clothing budget.

Clothing $ _____   [3]

Enter at [3] on page 92.

Food

Some years back, a TV commercial featured a well-known naturalist who asked that memorable question, "Ever eat a pine tree?" He went on to inform viewers that "Some parts are edible." Perhaps. But most of us have come to expect more sophisticated fare. Still, there's plenty of room for negotiation between grazing in the forest and living solely on steak and caviar. The government has defined four kinds of food plans, each of which supplies the necessary nutrients. The Thrifty Plan is based on low-cost foods (beans, rice), but these may be unappealing to some people and may take more time for preparation. The Moderate Plan offers a greater variety of foods. The Liberal Plan lets you buy whatever you want, regardless of the cost.

Would you like your diet to be based on:

☐ The Thrifty Plan   ☐ The Moderate Plan

☐ The Low-Cost Plan   ☐ The Liberal Plan

Do you have any special dietary habits that might increase your food budget (i.e., gourmet cooking is your hobby, you have a restricted diet)? The chart on page 85 may help you come up with an amount.

Food $ _____ [4]

Enter at [4] on page 92.

Sundries

Sundries are all those little things you pick up at the grocery or drug store: Shampoo, deodorant, toilet paper, cleaning supplies, and the like. How much would you plan to spend on these items each month?

Sundries $ _____ [5]

Enter at [5] on page 92.

The chart below is to help you come up with some estimated food costs. Pick the family size closest to the family profile you outlined on page 77 and then pick the type of food plan (thrifty, low-cost, moderate-cost, or liberal) you would prefer. If the sample family sizes don't match your profile, you can always add to your estimate using the individual costs.

COST OF FOOD AT HOME				
Per Month				
	Thrifty Plan	Low-Cost Plan	Moderate-Cost Plan	Liberal Plan
Family of 2 20–50 years	$325.50	$376.90	$514.60	$644.50
Family of 4 Couple & 2 Preschoolers	$525.50	$629.90	$828.00	$1,001.10
Couple & 2 School age	$598.90	$740.60	$974.30	$1,184.60
INDIVIDUALS				
Child:				
1 year	$88.20	$118.40	$135.40	$164.10
2 years	$95.30	$121.40	$146.70	$178.30
3–5 years	$100.00	$126.50	$156.70	$190.60
6–8 years	$127.10	$172.70	$212.30	$250.50
9–11 years	$146.30	$191.00	$247.40	$289.60
Male: 19–50 years	$172.40	$222.40	$277.50	$339.70
Female: 19–50 years	$153.10	$415.80	$237.10	$304.80

Source: U.S. Department of Agriculture, Family Economics and Nutrition Review, January 2011.

Entertainment and Recreation

Although the following budget items are not necessary to sustain life, they do have an impact on your self-esteem and life satisfaction. Answer the following questions, remembering to consider your spouse and your children's needs as well.

Monthly Total

How many times/month will you eat at a restaurant? _____

What will your average bill be? $ _____

How much per month will be spent on meals out? $ _____

Would you like to entertain friends?

What would you spend per month? $ _____

Would you like to attend concerts, movies, plays, sports events, and the like?

What would you spend per month? $ _____

Will you buy download music or mobile apps? Subscribe to newspapers and magazines on your e-book reader?

How much a month would you like to spend? $ _____

Will you have hobbies or take part in sports that cost money?

What? _____

How much will you need a month? $ _____

If you have children, what kinds of recreational/educational opportunities do you want for them? (Check their ages again.)

What? _____

How much will be spent per month? $ _____

One more consideration: Do you want to have special equipment related to entertainment or recreation? Would you like to have a laptop or tablet computer, MP3 player, gaming system, HDTV, musical instrument, boat, plane, country club or health club membership?

What do you want to spend on them per month? $ _____

Total entertainment $ _____ [6]

Enter at [6] on page 92.

Vacations

This is not so much a "whether or not" budget item as it is a "where and how often" expenditure. It's been shown that taking time off is an important part of maintaining good physical and mental health. How do you want to do it?

Do you want to take a vacation:

☐ Monthly

☐ Every six months

☐ Yearly

☐ Every two years

☐ Every three to five years

☐ Other _____

What kind of vacation would you like to be able to afford:

☐ Car trip to relatives

☐ Camping/hiking

☐ Day trips to local amusements

☐ A week at the seashore or mountain cabin

☐ Car trips to places of interest

☐ Plane trips to places of interest

☐ Foreign travel

☐ Cruises, travel packages, or exotic clubs

☐ Other _____

☐ Other _____

☐ Other _____

What will you want to budget every year to meet your vacation objectives? $ _____

Divide that figure by 12 to come up with your monthly figure.

Vacation $ _____ [7]

Enter at [7] on page 92.

Child Care

If both parents are working while there are young children in the family (a reasonable assumption), you will need to consider your child care options. First, look back to see how many children you are planning to have, and their ages.

Would you have:

☐ No need for child care

☐ A relative to care for them

☐ A cooperative arrangement with a relative or friend

☐ Care in a community-based center

☐ A private nursery school or day care center

☐ A sitter coming into your home

☐ Live-in help

NATIONAL AVERAGE CHILD CARE COSTS	
Babysitter (in home, non-relative) Source: U.S. Census Bureau	$9.25/hour
Average Weekly Child Care Costs at Child Care Center	
Infant	$172.57
4-year-old child	$137.60
School-age child	$94.96

Source: Figures extrapolated from state averages, National Association of Child Care Resources & Referral Agencies, 2008 Price of Child Care, March 2009.

How much will this cost per child, per month?

child one $ _____

child two $ _____

child three $ _____

Total child care costs $ _____ [8]

Enter at [8] on page 92.

DEPENDANT CARE

If you indicated at the beginning of this exercise that you plan to care for a dependant other than your children (a parent or grandparent, for example) remember to add that into your monthly budget. What do you plan to spend on dependant care? $ _____

What if there is a divorce of separation in your future? Will you need to pay alimony or child support? How much? $ _____ Keep these costs in mind as you plan for monthly reserves.

Health Care

Because an unforeseen accident or illness can play havoc with the most carefully planned budget, health insurance is a must. Many employers will subsidize your health insurance. But usually you will have to pay a portion of the cost. What kind of care do you want?

- ☐ Government-subsidized free clinics
- ☐ Health Maintenance Organization care
- ☐ Private physician and dentist

See page 94 for some sample annual costs. Divide your projected annual costs by 12 months.

Health Care $ _____ [9]

Enter at [9] on page 92.

Furnishings

You probably need to purchase replacement equipment and items for your home, such as linens, appliances, furniture, and decorative items. What about computer or home entertainment equipment? Assume you have most of these items by this time.

Annual budget $ _____ divided by 12.

Furnishings $ _____ [10]

Enter at [10] on page 92.

Savings

This is an important part of any budget. There are predictable things to save for (a house, new furnishings, children's college, retirement) as well as things you'd rather not think about (losing your job, a major illness). It's not fun to spend money on a new roof or water heater, but sometimes it has to be done. And, it's a lot easier if you've planned for it. As a rule of thumb, every family should save at least six months' income in case of emergency.

What do you feel you should save each month for:

- ☐ Emergencies
- ☐ Repairs, replacements, or major purchases
- ☐ Children's college
- ☐ Retirement
- ☐ Income cushion

Savings $ _____ [11]

Enter at [11] on page 92.

Miscellaneous

Are there things important to you that we haven't mentioned yet? Think about your values. Here are some possible additional expenses. Add your own if you need to.

What will be your monthly budget for holiday gifts and birthdays? $ _____

Will you have pets? If so, what kind? _____

How much per month will it cost to keep them? $ _____

Will you make contributions to social, political, or religious organizations?
If so, how much per month? $ _____

Do you want to send your children to private schools?   Yes   No   Undecided

How much will this cost per month? $ _____

Do you need an Internet connection, cable TV, cell phone, or other high tech services?

How much will this cost per month? $ _____

Other costs, list: _____ $ _____

_____ $ _____

_____ $ _____

Miscellaneous $ _____ [12]

Enter at [12] on page 92.

My
10yearPlan
.com

ESTIMATED COST OF RAISING A CHILD
Birth to 17 years old

Income Group	Estimated Total Expenditure
Lowest: less than $56,670*	$205,960
Middle: $56,670 to $98,120	$286,050
Highest: greater than $98,120	$475,680

* Income figures are based on total pre-tax household incomes.

Source: U.S. Department of Agriculture, *Expenditures on Children by Families,* 2009, June 2010.

If you save $100 per month at a specific interest, you will have in:					
	4%	6%	8%	10%	12%
5 years	$ 6,630	$ 6,977	$ 7,348	$ 7,743	$ 8,167
10 years	$14,725	$16,388	$18,295	$20,484	$23,004
15 years	$24,609	$29,082	$34,604	$41,447	$49,958
20 years	$36,677	$46,204	$58,902	$75,937	$98,926

AVERAGE ANNUAL COLLEGE COSTS
by type of institution

	Public 4-Year	Private 4-Year	Public 2-Year	Private 2-Year
Tuition & Room/Board	$14,256	$31,704	$7,567	$22,742
Tuition/Required Fees (in-state)	$6,319	$22,449	$2,137	$13,632
Dormitory Rooms	$4,322	$5,041	$2,654	$4,519
Board (7-day basis)	$3,616	$4,214	$2,777	$4,591

Source: U.S. Department of Education, National Center for Education Statistics, Digest of Education Statistics: 2009, April 2010.

Your Budget Profile

Here's the moment of truth. Go through the exercise again and enter the monthly amounts you indicated in each category in the appropriate space below. Then add the column to come up with your total monthly budget.

[1] Housing $ _____

[2] Transportation $ _____

[3] Clothing $ _____

[4] Food $ _____

[5] Sundries $ _____

[6] Entertainment $ _____

[7] Vacations $ _____

[8] Child care $ _____

[9] Health care $ _____

[10] Furnishings $ _____

[11] Savings $ _____

[12] Miscellaneous $ _____

   Total $ _____

My
10yearPlan
.com

What Salary Will Support this Lifestyle?

The figure you have just computed is the total amount of money you will need to bring home in your paycheck. But you will need to earn more money than this figure because of deductions from your paycheck for Social Security, state, and federal taxes.

So before you begin looking for a career, you need to figure the gross pay (salary) needed to meet your budget requirements.

Taxing authorities use precise calculations to factor deductions. For the sake of this exercise, figure an average of 20% is withheld from your paycheck. What you have after taxes have been withheld is called net pay or takehome pay. This is the amount of money you have left to cover your expenses.

To find the monthly salary you will need to cover your expenses, divide your monthly expenses by 80 percent.

Expenses (or net pay) divided by 80% = Gross pay

_____ ÷ 80% = _____
Total from page 92   your required monthly salary

Multiply this figure by 12 (months) to get the annual salary figure required.

_____ x 12 = _____
your required monthly salary   your required annual salary

Keep this figure in mind as you start researching career possibilities. You might start by reading the employment section of classified advertisements in both your local newspaper and the newspaper of the closest large city or visit local online employment web sites. Do the jobs that meet your financial needs sound interesting?

AVERAGE ANNUAL INCOME				
	One Person	Two Persons	Three Persons	Four Persons	Five or More Persons
Income before taxes	$32,780	$68,393	$76,545	$85,436	$80,132

SOURCE: U.S. Bureau of Labor Statistics, Consumer Expenditures in 2009, October 2010.

What Careers Support Your Lifestyle?

As you continue your life planning and career decision-making process, a key task is to find a career that will support the lifestyle you envision for yourself AND for which you think you will be qualified.

Keep your required annual salary figure from page 93 in mind as you start researching career possibilities in chapter six. You might start by browsing the jobs that are available in your area on a job search web site. Or, check out the employment listings in the classified section of both your local newspaper and a paper in the closest large city. There are also online classified services that accept listings for employment opportunities, the most famous of which is CraigsList.

Consult the Occupational Outlook Handbook * (OOH). Each job title listed has extensive earnings information. The Bureau of Labor Statistics has made the entire OOH available online in an easy-to-use format or you can find a copy at your local library or bookstore.

Using your favorite Internet search engine, such as Yahoo, Google, or Bing, you can locate other online compensation and salary resources by using the keyword "salary" and adding the job title of a specific career you want to investigate (e.g., salary + commercial diver).

To find those occupations that match your financial and lifestyle requirements, be prepared to spend some time exploring a variety of options. Make a list below of at least ten careers with average salaries that match your budget projections. For this activity, assume you are the sole "breadwinner" in your family.

CAREER TITLE AND AVERAGE SALARY

_____

_____

_____

_____

CAREER TITLE AND AVERAGE SALARY

_____

_____

_____

_____

* At the time of printing, the web address was http://www.bls.gov/oco

In Over Your Head?

As much as we would sometimes like to ignore them, numbers don't lie. You may be surprised at many of the costs. If your budget total seems unreasonably high, you will need to make some adjustments.

Go back and review your figures. Where could you make cuts most easily? Write your adjusted figures in a different color pen or pencil. These numbers should add up to the minimum amount of money you need to lead a lifestyle that would be acceptable to you.

Roberta, for example, decided that the several hundred dollars a month she could save by giving up her dream luxury car for a more modest vehicle wouldn't really be painful. It may be a bit depressing to adjust your dreams downward, but being a slave to your lifestyle isn't fun, either.

Bob and Barbara, like many people, found themselves "house poor." They dreamed of having a big new house in the best part of town. They built it, but the mortgage payments are so high that there's no money left for little pleasures like an occasional dinner and movie in town. Several years of living in anxiety because of their over-stretched budget has taken its toll on their health, their marriage, and their life satisfaction.

When Jason lost his job, he decided to get a roommate to share expenses. He found he could make ends meet by cutting out most recreational expenses and adjusting his eating habits: No steak for a while, lots of spaghetti.

Back to your budget. Did the figure you arrived at on page 92 seem higher than the salary you're likely to earn on your own? What amount do you think you could reasonably expect to earn? Write that figure on line b below.

Next, determine your net income (line a), if you earn that salary (see formula on page 93).

Now, reallocate your funds. Write the adjusted figures for your hard times budget below. The total should be a figure no larger than your *own* income. Don't count on your phantom spouse here.

HARD TIMES BUDGET

1. Housing $ _____

2. Transportation $ _____

3. Clothing $ _____

4. Food $ _____

5. Sundries $ _____

6. Entertainment $ _____

7. Vacations $ _____

8. Child care $ _____

9. Health care $ _____

10. Furnishings $ _____

11. Savings $ _____

12. Miscellaneous $ _____

a) Net Income $ _____
(total amount you have to spend)

b) Gross monthly salary $ _____
(amount you expect to earn)

Some Sample Budgets

Phyllis, a single mother of two, teaches English at a high school in Southern California. Her sons are twelve and ten years old. The family lives in a small house in one of the older sections of town. It's a long drive to work for Phyllis, but new housing is very expensive. Besides, they like their old neighborhood. The boys attend a magnet school where they are getting an early chance to excel at languages and math. Every Friday night, the whole family goes out for pizza. Phyllis's hobby is photography, and she recently purchased a digital camera. Every summer, the family takes a two-week car trip to a place where Phyllis can take photos and the boys can enjoy and learn.

PHYLLIS'S BUDGET

1.	Housing	$ 1,610
2.	Transportation	$ 370
3.	Clothing	$ 300
4.	Food	$ 495
5.	Sundries	$ 50
6.	Entertainment	$ 100
7.	Vacations	$ 85
8.	Child care	$ 35
9.	Health care	$ 300
10.	Furnishings	$ 70
11.	Savings	$ 230
12.	Miscellaneous	$ 90
	Net Income	$ 3,735

What is the gross monthly income required to come up with this net? $ _____

Will has been in the army for three years. The pay's not great, but since he's single and doesn't have to pay for room or board, he has no complaints. Will loves to travel—that's one reason he enlisted. He saves part of every check for his travel fund, in order to take advantage of the special prices he can get while he's in the service. Last year he spent a month in Europe. This year he wants to go to Japan. Will recently opened another savings account to save money for a new car.

WILL'S BUDGET

1.	Housing	$ _____
2.	Transportation	$ _____
3.	Clothing	$ _____
4.	Food	$ _____
5.	Sundries	$ _____
6.	Entertainment	$ _____
7.	Vacations	$ _____
8.	Child care	$ _____
9.	Health care	$ _____
10.	Furnishings	$ _____
11.	Savings	$ _____
12.	Miscellaneous	$ _____
	Net Income	$ _____1,700_____

What is the gross monthly income required to come up with this net? $ _____

Jeff and Francie and their two kids live in a new housing development in Indiana. Jeff works at a nearby factory, where he's been employed for 15 years. Francie works in the office at the plant. The twins are 14. They're bright kids, and Jeff and Francie want to send them to college. They were worried a few years ago when many people at the factory were laid off, but Jeff and Francie both kept their jobs. The children's college fund is intact and growing. When the family goes on vacation, their main concern is getting out of the city. Usually they go camping or rent a cabin on a lake. Francie says it seems like that's about the only time the whole family does anything together anymore—the boys are busy with part-time jobs and afterschool activities. But she and Jeff have started going out alone a couple times a month, something they both enjoy.

JEFF & FRANCIE'S BUDGET

1. Housing $ _____

2. Transportation $ _____

3. Clothing $ _____

4. Food $ _____

5. Sundries $ _____

6. Entertainment $ _____

7. Vacations $ _____

8. Child care $ _____

9. Health care $ _____

10. Furnishings $ _____

11. Savings $ _____

12. Miscellaneous $ _____

        Net Income $ _____3,300_____

Total: $2,200/month take-home salary, Jeff
            $1,100/month take-home salary, Francie

What is the gross monthly income required to come up with this net? $ _____

Carl is a psychologist and Ruth is a bank executive. They live with their small daughter in a cooperative apartment in New York City. Since their careers call for long and unpredictable hours at work, they have live-in help for the baby. They don't have a car—most of the time it's not necessary. They rent one when they need to. Vacations have been fewer since the baby was born, but the family would someday like a weekend cottage in the country. The full-time babysitter also makes it easier for Carl and Ruth to go out at night. They both love the theater and enjoy trying out new restaurants.

CARL & RUTH'S BUDGET

1. Housing $ _____
2. Transportation $ _____
3. Clothing $ _____
4. Food $ _____
5. Sundries $ _____
6. Entertainment $ _____
7. Vacations $ _____
8. Child care $ _____
9. Health care $ _____
10. Furnishings $ _____
11. Savings $ _____
12. Miscellaneous $ _____

Net Income $ _____11,500_____

Total: $5,200/month take-home salary, Carl
$6,300/month take-home salary, Ruth

What is the gross monthly income required to come up with this net? $ _____

Ben is a golf pro in Fort Lauderdale. Lynn is a nurse, but she's been home full-time since the birth of their first child. The family has a ranch house in the suburbs, with a big yard for the kids (now four and seven) and a garden for Lynn. They have two cars, neither of them new, but both kept in good condition by Ben. Outings are usually casual events like picnics at the beach. They like to have friends over for barbecue. Since Ben knows golf pros all over the country, vacation time means swapping homes with another family—a different part of the country each year. This year, they're all looking forward to a stay in Colorado.

BEN & LYNN'S BUDGET

1. Housing $ _____

2. Transportation $ _____

3. Clothing $ _____

4. Food $ _____

5. Sundries $ _____

6. Entertainment $ _____

7. Vacations $ _____

8. Child care $ _____

9. Health care $ _____

10. Furnishings $ _____

11. Savings $ _____

12. Miscellaneous $ _____

Net Income $ _____3,190_____

What is the gross monthly income required to come up with this net? $ _____

A Few Words about Poverty

Though the United States is one of the richest nations on earth, millions of its citizens today are living in poverty. Many of these are homeless, living in shelters or on the street, often reduced to begging for quarters or going through garbage cans in order to eat. For many others, a majority of them women, children, and the elderly, life offers little more than anxiety about paying the rent or buying the groceries they need. The societal and historical forces that have caused this situation must be changed, but that will take time.

How can you assure that you will not be a future poverty statistic? There are no guarantees, but here are some things you might think about:

> If you are female, be aware of the fact that, on average, women earn only 81 cents for every dollar earned by a man. Part of this discrepancy is due to discrimination. Part of it is a result of women clustering in career fields such as teaching, retail, and clerical work that, as a rule, are not high paying.

> Another problem is that women grow up believing that someone else will take care of them. They do not adequately prepare for a job because they do not believe that they will ever *have* to have one.

If you are a woman, and if you are still in school, one of the best things you can do to ensure your future is to take math, science, and technology classes, and do as well in them as you can. If you have any skills and interests related to traditionally male careers, pursue them. Even though a woman engineer may not earn as much as a male engineer, she almost certainly will make more than a bookkeeper or secretary.

Assume that you *will* have to support yourself. Plan for that eventuality and, if it comes about, at least you will be prepared.

Could You Become a Poverty Statistic?

Approximately 43,600,000 people in the United States live below the poverty level. That is 14.3 percent of the total population.

9.2 percent of all families live below the poverty level.

About 19 percent of American households are headed by a woman.

29.9 percent of all families headed by a woman with no husband present live below the poverty level.

In the United States, 19 percent of all children live below the poverty level.

Single-parent families maintained by men have median weekly earnings of $802. Single-parent families maintained by women have median weekly earnings of $558. Married-couple families have median weekly earnings of $1,404.

What do you think contributes to poverty in this country?

_____

_____

_____

What might cause you to become one of these statistics?

_____

_____

How can you prevent that from happening?

_____

_____

_____

Source: U.S. Census Bureau, Current Population Reports, *Income, Poverty, and Health Insurance Coverage in the United States: 2009*, Washington, DC, 2010.

Money Isn't Everything

On the other hand, it's quite possible to put more emphasis on money than it deserves: If only we were rich and famous, we think, we'd certainly be happy. But would we? Every day, it seems, there is news of one more celebrity getting divorced, being treated for drug addiction or alcoholism or emotional illness, or even committing suicide.

We won't attempt to say why this is so, but the stories do demonstrate that wealth and fame do not guarantee a rewarding life. The status symbols—the cars and houses and jewelry and so on—are very effective at making other people envious. However, they often mean little to their owners.

Studies have shown that people with a comfortable income are usually much happier than those living in poverty. But excessive amounts of money do not seem to add significantly to life satisfaction.

Many people make conscious decisions to forego higher incomes in order to do something they think is more worthwhile, such as teaching. Besides their service to society, teachers value other benefits such as the vacation time to pursue other interests or be with their families.

A well-paid advertising executive who really wants to write short stories may be less satisfied with her life than a bus driver who loves his job. That is why it is so important to consider your values when making career decisions. Go back to the values exercise on page 35 and review which values are most important to you. Whatever course you take in your life must be compatible with them.

Every job has psychological and emotional costs. The trick is to find a balance: that is, a job that pays enough to support the kind of *physical* lifestyle you want, while not draining your *spirit* by forcing you to deny those values you hold most dear.

Consider the following stories. What values are being sacrificed in each case? We've used Bert's story as an example.

> You will recall that our values categories are adventure, family, knowledge and truth, power, personal integrity and moral courage, money or wealth, friendship and companionship, recognition, independence and freedom, security, beauty or aesthetics, creativity, and helping others.

BERT'S STORY

I've wanted to be a missionary ever since I was a boy. Every year, people would come to our church from some distant country and show slides and talk about the work they were doing for the people there. I love to travel, and my religion has always been important to me. Right now, I'm stationed on an island in the South Pacific. We're building a new school and a much-needed hospital. It's taking longer than it should because sometimes the money just doesn't come through. It's difficult when your only support comes from people who are thousands of miles away. I have to remind myself to have faith and that, so far, things have always worked out. The people here are wonderful and they've taught me so much. I never thought I could be so thrilled about getting a bar of soap or a box of chocolate in the mail. Last time I was home I went into a supermarket and just stared at all the variety—the sheer number of things you can just pick up and buy. They even carry it to your car for you! But that was three years ago. I haven't seen my family since then. I'm not sure when I'll be sent somewhere else, and that makes it hard, but I think we've really accomplished something for the people on this island, and that makes it all worthwhile.

What are the sacrifices Bert must make?

Time away from his family, little access to material goods, dependence on others for support, not in control of his own future

Which values do those sacrifices reflect?

Family, money and wealth, security

What are his rewards?

Feeling like he's making a difference, being surrounded by people he respects

Which values do they reflect?

Personal integrity and moral courage, friendship and companionship, helping others

Do you share some of Bert's values?   Yes   No   Undecided

Are you willing to make similar sacrifices?   Yes   No   Undecided

If so, you may be happy with a career like Bert's.

LEON'S STORY

All I have to do to remind myself of the power I hold is to walk through the halls of this company. Five thousand employees, and they all know I could promote them or give them a raise—or fire them on the spot. I like the way everyone smiles and calls me "Sir" and goes out of the way to try to please me. I guess it sounds as though I'm just on a power trip, but I've worked hard to build this company and earn the respect of the people who work here. When I think of all the years of 60 or 80 hours a week in the office, all the kids' birthday parties I missed, the anniversaries I forgot. . . . Well, maybe it's no wonder that I don't get the same respect at home that I do at work. The kids are grown now, and I feel that I hardly know them. My wife has built a life of her own, and I'm not exactly indispensable to her. But I love the job. I plan to stay here as long as my health holds out—maybe until I'm 75.

What are the sacrifices Leon must make?

_____

Which values do these sacrifices reflect?

_____

What are Leon's rewards?

_____

Which values do they reflect?

_____

Do you share Leon's values?   Yes   No   Undecided

Are you willing to make the same sacrifices?   Yes   No   Undecided

If so, you might be happy with a similar career.

VINCENT'S STORY

Yesterday I sold my first painting. You might think that after all those years when no one was interested, selling one painting wouldn't mean very much. You would be wrong. It's not the recognition or the money I'm after. I see such incredible beauty in the world, and I only want to find a way to express it and to share it. I've had to take many jobs over the years—cab driver, hospital orderly, janitor—but I've never thought of myself as anything but an artist.

What are the sacrifices Vincent has made?

_____

_____

Which values do they reflect?

_____

_____

What are Vincent's rewards?

_____

_____

Which values do they reflect?

_____

_____

Do you share Vincent's values?   Yes   No   Undecided

Would you be ready to make similar sacrifices?

                                    Yes   No   Undecided

If so, you might be happy with a similar career.

SARA'S STORY

Being an environmental scientist is one of the most important jobs I can think of. After all, this is the only planet we have. I really love my job and I don't take the responsibility lightly. I had no social life in school because I was so serious about my studies. But, truthfully, I've always preferred books to parties. The thing is, I'm still studying. There's always something new to learn. I hardly ever see anyone away from work. I can't remember the last time I went shopping or played a round of golf. I've always wanted to have children, but that plan is on hold for now. Last week, though, we learned that fish have returned to a river I helped clean up and—well, you don't get a feeling like that from an afternoon of shopping. It's not easy, but I'm proud of what I do.

What sacrifices has Sara had to make? _____

_____

_____

What values categories would you put them under? _____

_____

_____

List Sara's rewards. _____

_____

_____

To which values categories do they belong? _____

_____

Do you and Sara have similar values?   Yes   No   Undecided

Would you be willing to make the same sacrifices?

                                             Yes   No   Undecided

If so, this might be a career for you to think about.

ROSE'S STORY

I've always had two goals: To have a good family life, and to be successful at a career. I love to travel. For a while I thought I might be a pilot, but that would mean being away from home a lot. I'm pretty good at math, too, and I'm a stickler for details, so I decided to become an accountant. I worked for a big firm for a few years, until Allen and I decided to start a family. Then I opened my own office at home. It's not as prestigious, but since I can control the number of clients I take on, I was able to scale the job down when the children were small and spend most of my time with them. Now that they're in school all day, I work full-time. I'm the boss, though, so I can arrange my schedule in order to be there for special events at school or when somebody's home sick. Allen has a good job, too, but it's important to me to know that I could support the family on my own if I had to.

What sacrifices has Rose made for her career? _____

_____

What values categories would you place them in? _____

_____

What are her rewards? _____

_____

What values do you think they mirror? _____

_____

Are your values similar to Rose's?   Yes   No   Undecided

Would you make the same sacrifices?   Yes   No   Undecided

If so, a career like hers might make you happy.

You Win Some, You Lose Some

Every job has its rewards and its sacrifices. How well a given career could work for you depends on your own values. It's important to recognize which values are compatible with a job and which are not. See how adept you are at recognizing which traits a job will call forth, and which it will deny. Review the values categories on pages 36 and 37. Then, for each of the following careers, list the values you think will be rewarded and those that will most likely be sacrificed.

Example: Career Military Officer

Rewards: <u>Adventure</u>

Sacrifices: <u>Freedom, money or wealth</u>

Computer programmer

Rewards: <u>Security, creativity</u>

Sacrifices: <u>Beauty and aesthetics, adventure</u>

Professional athlete

Rewards: <u>Recognition, power, adventure</u>

Sacrifices: <u>Freedom, security</u>

Fire fighter
Rewards: _____

Sacrifices: _____

Veterinarian
Rewards: _____

Sacrifices: _____

Fashion model
Rewards: _____

Sacrifices: _____

Radio announcer
Rewards: _____

Sacrifices: _____

Social worker
Rewards: _____

Sacrifices: _____

Mechanic
Rewards: _____

Sacrifices: _____

Farmer
Rewards: _____

Sacrifices: _____

Truck driver
Rewards: _____

Sacrifices: _____

Flight attendant
Rewards: _____

Sacrifices: _____

Homemaker
Rewards: _____

Sacrifices: _____

Garbage hauler
Rewards: _____

Sacrifices: _____

Accountant
Rewards: _____

Sacrifices: _____

Resort owner
Rewards: _____

Sacrifices: _____

After Hours Rewards

Perhaps you found it difficult to determine which values the preceding jobs would not satisfy. There are several possible explanations, if you did. First of all, we generally look only at the rewards (financial and emotional) a given career has to offer. Personal and spiritual sacrifices are seldom mentioned, if they are even perceived. Also, some sacrifices don't become immediately apparent. In some cases, they may not appear at all. Anything from your individual employer to the economic situation of the world can affect the way you feel about your job.

As a result, many people end up in careers they've trained for, but that don't satisfy all their values. What can you do about that? Well, you can always change jobs, but sometimes there are powerful reasons to stay put. For example, a college professor who has invested many years in education may well hesitate before chucking it all to become a dancer just because teaching doesn't satisfy her creative side. Sometimes the job market is so bleak that anyone with any kind of job feels lucky. Or, if you have three children to support, you may have to pass on what could be your last chance to play minor league baseball because the wage is minimal.

Does that mean you're doomed to a lifetime of misery or, at best, of vague dissatisfaction? Not at all. Work may represent a sizeable chunk of your life, but it has no claim on your free time. Many people have found after-hours activities to fill in and make amends for those things that are lacking from 9 to 5.

Daniel is a garbage hauler. His top values are security and power. The job pays well, and it is certainly secure. ("One thing we know for sure," his boss is fond of saying, "there will always be garbage.") But power? Not much evidence of that. One day while Daniel was teaching his daughter how to throw a fastball, a neighbor stopped by, watched awhile, and suggested that Daniel might make a good Little League coach. He knew of a team that needed one. Daniel said, "Why not," and he's been having a great time leading his team to glory ever since.

Maria is an electrical engineer. Her top values are security, recognition, and aesthetics. Engineering met her need for security, but didn't satisfy her other requirements. She didn't want to give up her job, but she needed more satisfaction in her life. Maria decided to join a community theater group. She loves the atmosphere, she loves the plays, and most of all, she loves the applause.

Rodrigo is the executive director of a youth-service agency. Security and helping others are his top values. The job was great—he didn't want to leave it—but the pay was low and unlikely to improve. He couldn't save any money, and that made him feel insecure. When he received a small windfall from his grandmother, he decided to put it to work. He studied about investments and real estate, found some friends interested in a joint venture, and made some long-term plans. By investing wisely, Rodrigo was able to build an account for his retirement or for financial emergencies that might occur.

On each of the following lines, you'll find an occupation followed by a list of values. Circle those values you think would be met by the career. Then, on the line provided, state what this person might do to meet the other need.

Social worker: helping others   creativity   power _____

Assembly line worker: helping others   security   friendship _____

Carpenter: adventure   beauty and aesthetics   family _____

Sales representative: family   money   friendship _____

Homemaker: family   helping others   power _____

Museum guide: beauty and aesthetics   adventure   creativity _____

Professor: knowledge   creativity   recognition _____

Farmer: family   helping others   friendship _____

Psychologist: adventure   helping others   beauty and aesthetics _____

Accountant: power   money   creativity _____

Chemist: knowledge   creativity   recognition _____

Writer: creativity   helping others   friendship _____

Veterinarian: helping others   knowledge   power _____

Commitment

In high school, David, Michael, and Diane were inseparable. They agreed that music was the most important thing in the world. All were gifted musicians, and the threesome could always be found in the music room at school, at the record store, or at the back stage entrance to Orchestra Hall. They loved all kinds of music—rock, jazz, classical, country, hip hop—and they vowed that, somehow, music would always be at the center of their lives.

After graduation, David attended a college with one of the best music programs in the country. Because of his excellent work there, he was awarded a fellowship to continue his studies in Europe. His dedication to his art eventually led to a job with one of the most prestigious orchestras in the U.S.

Diane took a different track. While in college, she began singing with a local rock group. She and one of the other musicians started writing songs together. The rest of the group eventually fell apart, but Diane and her partner formed and reformed the band, playing anywhere they could get a job, sometimes without pay. They spent years auditioning, posting demos on YouTube, trying to get noticed, and—most of all—working to improve their music. The band recently signed with an agent, and Diane hopes they will have a recording contract soon.

Michael didn't see much point in continuing his education after high school. Convinced that he would be the next country music superstar, he headed directly to Nashville and tried very hard—for about a week—to get discovered. Well, he thought, maybe he'd rather be a song writer, anyway. He dashed off two sets of lyrics and sent them to his favorite singer. When there was no response, Michael got angry. "Who wants to be part of an arrogant industry like this, anyway," he reassured himself as he tried to hitch a ride home. He'd be much happier working for his uncle's construction company, a place where he'd surely be appreciated.

As the above story demonstrates, ability alone will not make you successful. In the end, whether or not you *can* do something may be less important than how much you *want* to do it, how committed you are to achieving your goal.

Lots of people have dreams. But, like Michael, many people are unwilling to put in the necessary work to make their dreams come true. David and Diane did not succeed through luck, but through persistence and hard work. What kind of persistence would it take to realize *your* dream?

While most jobs require some kind of commitment toward training or education, the amount varies. You can probably get a beginning clerical position with only a high school business class. To be a psychiatrist, however, you have to go through college and medical school before you even *begin* your psychiatric training. That's quite a commitment—of time, energy, and money.

Similarly, some careers require continued commitment. It may be possible to be a casual or part-time sales clerk, but it is difficult to imagine an uncommitted professional tennis player or member of Congress.

Often, the financial dividends and independence make the investment of time and effort worthwhile. Professionals like doctors and lawyers are among the highest-paid people in our society. In most careers, the person who is most committed to the work—the one who has taken time to learn more or perform better—is the one likely to reach the top of the pay scale.

However, there are no guarantees. Dancers and musicians, for example, may train for many years and still never earn a living from their art. They "do it for love," realizing that the odds are against them.

Before choosing your career, it's important to consider the degree of commitment you feel comfortable with—both in training and on-the-job performance. Some people want their work to be a dominant force in their lives. For others, it is important to have plenty of time for family and other interests.

Again, there is no right or wrong answer. The choice is yours. The following exercise will give you a better idea of how an investment of time and/or money relates to future dividends.

An Investment in Education...

An investment in your future begins with education: The amount of time you are willing to devote to your training, the kinds of classes you are willing to take, and the amount of work you are willing to do in those classes. If you take math and science courses in high school (and do well in them), you will have more options concerning where you will go to college and what you will major in once you get there. Reading and writing skills are also essential in most career fields. College, of course, means more time committed. But, in general, time devoted to education will pay off in the long run.

The following chart demonstrates the relationship between time commitment and financial reward.

JOB TITLE	MEDIAN ANNUAL EARNINGS	POST HIGH SCHOOL TRAINING/EDUCATION
Brickmason	$44,758	144 hours classroom instruction + 3-year apprenticeship
Court Reporter	$49,710	2 to 4 years
Medical Transcriptionist	$31,436	1-year certificate or 2-year degree
Respiratory Therapist	$52,200	2-year degree + exam
Plumber	$44,758	4- or 5-year apprenticeship + annual classroom instruction
Elementary School Teacher	$47,100	4 years college + 1 year post graduate
Computer Programmer	$69,620	2 to 4 years
Computer Systems Analyst	$75,500	4+ years
Air Traffic Controller	$111,870	3 to 4 years school and/or work experience + exam
School Psychologist	$65,710	9 to 11 years
Chemical Engineer	$74,600	4-year degree or more
College Professor (full professor)	$108,479	6 to 8 years
Chiropractor (salaried)	$66,490	6 to 8 years + exam
Dentist	$142,870	6 to 8 years + exam
Attorney	$110,590	7 years + passage of bar exam
Physician (primary care)	$186,044	11 to 16 years

Amounts reflect national median earnings, assuming full-time work.
Source: U.S. Department of Labor, Bureau of Labor Statistics, *Occupational Outlook Handbook,* 2010–2011 Edition.

...Yields Dividends for a Lifetime

While it may not seem that $10,000 or $20,000 per year earning capacity is a big enough inducement to spend between three and 10 more years in school or in training, let's look at what that extra effort can mean over a lifetime.

The chart below shows more dramatically how each year of education affects future earnings.

How many years do you plan to work between the age of 18 and 65?

_____ years in workforce

Multiply the number of years you plan to be in the workforce with each of the annual salaries listed below to find out how much you would earn over the course of your working life.

$20,000 x _____ years in workforce = $ _____ lifetime earnings

$30,000 x _____ years in workforce = $ _____ lifetime earnings

$50,000 x _____ years in workforce = $ _____ lifetime earnings

$75,000 x _____ years in workforce = $ _____ lifetime earnings

$100,000 x _____ years in workforce = $ _____ lifetime earnings

What is the difference between a $20,000 and $30,000 annual salary over a lifetime? $ _____

What is the difference between a $20,000 and $50,000 annual salary over a lifetime? $ _____

What is the difference between a $20,000 and $75,000 annual salary over a lifetime? $ _____

What is the difference between a $20,000 and $100,000 annual salary over a lifetime? $ _____

What if you only earned minimum wage?

What is the current minimum wage (rate per hour) in your state or city? $ _____

How much can a person earn per year at that hourly rate? $ _____

What does that equal over your lifetime? $ _____

117

HOW DO YOU WANT TO SPEND YOUR TIME?

Maybe the time required to get the education and training for a job that interests you still seems too long, higher income or no. Let's look at it another way.

This bar graph represents an average lifespan—about 78 years. We've already filled it in for a high school graduate. That leaves you about 60 years to play around with. How will you spend that time?

Now envision your ideal future. How will you spend your time? Think about the kind of life you'd like to have, the job that appeals to you most, no matter how long the training required. Using the following directions as a guide, fill in the graph to age 78.

Using *polka dots,* fill in and label the block(s) of time for *post-high school training.*

Using *horizontal stripes,* fill in and label the block(s) of time for *working full-time* and diagonal lines for *working part-time.*

Using *stars,* fill in and label the block(s) of time *outside the workforce* for raising a family or retirement.

75

70

65

60

55

50

45

40

35

25

20

High School

15

Junior High School

10

Elementary School

5

Lifespan Graph

Use the information from your graph to answer the following questions.

How many years of post-high school training will you complete?

_____ years = a

How many years do you think you will work outside the home full-time?

_____ years = b

How many years do you think you will work outside the home part-time?

_____ years = c

Here are some interesting facts about your worklife.

How many hours might you work in your lifetime?

full-time   2,080 hours/year x _____ b = _____ f
part-time   1,000 hours/year x _____ c = _____ g

_____ f + _____ g = _____ hours you will work in your lifetime

That's a lot of time to be doing something that you do not find satisfying...that doesn't correspond to your values or passions...that doesn't meet your lifestyle desires.
Okay, let's look at it one more way.

For every year of post-high school education, you will work _____ years.

Hint: $\dfrac{b + c}{a}$ = _____ h

Next time you think, "I can't stay in school _____ more years! I didn't want to be a _____ anyway!" remember these figures. Education and training now are a small investment when you look at the long-range payoffs in life satisfaction.
Hang in there...you'll be glad you did!

It is never too late to be what you might have been.
— George Elliot

Ask Someone Who's Been There

The information in this book is necessarily more general than we'd like. You'll want to get specific answers to your questions. Interview three people (over age 29) in fields that interest you, adding their comments to your career resource files. The following questions will trigger a dialogue and lead to an in-depth understanding of each occupation.

NAME _____

OCCUPATION _____

HOW LONG IN THIS OCCUPATION? _____

How did you choose your occupation? _____
_____

Financially, does it let you live the way you prefer? _____
_____

If not, why not and what can you do about it? _____
_____

What rewards have you experienced? _____

(Listen carefully here. Keep the different values categories in mind.)

Values interpretation: _____

What sacrifices have you had to make for your career? _____

Values interpretation: _____

What kind of commitment does this career take in terms of:

Education _____

Energy/endurance _____

Stick-to-itiveness _____

If you had it to do over again, would you choose this career? _____

Why or why not? _____

Easier Said Than Done

As anyone who's ever vowed to lose weight or to save money knows, it's easier to *make* a commitment than it is to *keep* one. Long-term commitments are particularly hard to keep. In his book, *The Path of Least Resistance,* author Robert Fritz explains that, while it may be relatively easy to follow through at first, it is natural, over time, to fall back into comfortable old habits. Those who push on to meet their long-term goals or fulfill their dreams are usually those who have a clear vision of where they want to go or what they want to create.

By holding a picture in your mind of what it is you want, you will be better able to make the right decisions about your day-to-day actions. Should you study for the lit exam or go to the party? Well, what do you want? This is a key question, one you need to ask yourself often. It may be easier or more fun to go to the party. If you want to get into graduate school, however, you probably need to study for the test. Keeping your goal in mind will make it easier to decide.

> Kay wants to save money for college. Her friend wants Kay to go with her on a ski vacation.
>
> Jamal wants to do well at his weekend job. He feels like sleeping in on Saturday morning.
>
> Lee wants to be in the school play. The thought of auditioning for a part makes him anxious.
>
> Juanita wants to study art in France. Because of a scheduling problem, taking a French class would mean giving up her place in the school choir.

	It's easier to…	…than…	But what I want is…	…therefore, I will…
Kay Jamal Lee Juanita You				

Complete this chart for Kay, Jamal, Lee, and Juanita.

What do you want? Look back to the goals you set in chapter 3 and fill in the chart above. Use this model to help make day-to-day decisions about realizing your dreams.

Keep pace with the drummer you hear,
however measured or far away.

—Henry David Thoreau

I never did a day's work in my life—it was
all fun.
                                    — Thomas Alva Edison

CHAPTER FIVE

Your Ideal Career

There's more to consider than just the work

Gena was assigned to write a description of her ideal job for class. "I don't want you to tell me what the job is," Ms. Brown had instructed. "Just tell me where you'd like to work, who you'd like to work with, what you'd like to get from your job — things like that." Gena sat down at her desk, turned on her computer, chewed three sticks of gum, sent an e-mail message to her friend in Nova Scotia, updated her Facebook status, and made several important phone calls. By 9 P.M. it was clear to her that she had no idea what to write.

A clever young woman, Gena decided to ask other people for their opinions, and they were more than happy to tell her what to do.

"A good job would involve a lot of travel," her friend Paul said. "You don't want to get stuck in some office all day, every day."

"It would have to be a job that lets you meet interesting people," her sister offered.

"I don't know about that," said her dad. "Be your own boss. That's the ticket."

"Do that and you'll never get a good night's sleep again," her grandfather proclaimed. "What you want is a secure job with a solid company. Something you know you can count on."

"If you want to have a family, it would help to have flexible hours," her mother said.

"Who cares about that?" asked her friend Susan. "I say go for the big bucks!"

Gena reviewed her notes at her desk. At first she didn't know what to make of such an odd assortment of opinions. As she thought about them, though, they began to make sense. A career, she realized, involves many things that have nothing at all to do with the actual work, yet greatly affect how effective and satisfied a worker will be.

In a way, Gena decided, choosing a rewarding career is like building a successful softball team. Every member of the team has an important role to play. Good pitching is essential, but without solid hitting and defense, it won't get you into the play-offs. Likewise, a job that pays well but is unrewarding in other respects won't make you happy.

What kinds of things need to be considered? Gena looked back at the answers she'd collected and listed different categories. Traveling? That would involve the physical setting of a job, she decided. Working with interesting people seemed to relate to working conditions. Her father's comment about being her own boss, she felt, concerned relationships on the job. The security her grandfather urged on her related, she knew, to his values. Her mother was right—she definitely had to consider how her job would affect her family life. And, of course, there was the financial angle to consider.

Under each category, Gena listed the things that were most important to her. This was a good way to begin narrowing her career choices, she decided. And, if she used her imagination, she could come up with some new ideas, too. What jobs could she think of that would include as many elements from her list as possible? This just might be fun, she thought.

Before you start investigating specific careers, it's a good idea to consider the general characteristics you favor in a job. They can provide an outline that will make your career research much easier. If you know you want to live in the city, for example, you can cross "forest ranger" right off your list of possible careers. Similarly, if you decide you want a job that lets you put family responsibilities first, you probably won't want to be a foreign correspondent for a network newscast.

On each of the following pages, you will find a brief description of a particular category of career considerations. A list of options involving that category follows. Check the box in front of any statement that appeals to you. Choose as many options as you like, but make sure they don't contradict each other. Feel free to add to the lists if we've overlooked something that appeals to you.

Physical Settings

By the setting of a job, we mean its geographic location as well as its specific working environment. Job satisfaction depends greatly on how you feel about where you work—and where your job forces you to live. You might love farming in the Midwest, for example. But if you have asthma or severe allergies, the humidity and pollen in the air could make your life miserable. Similarly, if you value beautiful surroundings, you probably won't want to work at a meat processing plant or a medical laboratory. And, if you can't stand to be indoors all day, a windowless inner office is not for you. Check the statements that appeal to you below.

☐ I would like to work in a city.

☐ I would like to work in the country.

☐ I would like to work in a small to medium-sized town.

☐ I would like to work in _____ (list a specific city or part of the country).

☐ I would like to work in another country _____ .

☐ I would like a job that might offer frequent transfers.

☐ I would like a job that will let me stay in one place.

☐ I would like a job that keeps me "on the road," traveling from place to place.

☐ I would like to work outdoors (list specifics if you can, i.e., in the woods, on a farm, at sea) _____ .

☐ I would like to work out of a car or truck most of the time.

☐ I would like to work in an office.

☐ I would like to work in my home.

☐ It's important to me that my work setting be pleasing to the eye.

☐ I would like to work in a garage or warehouse.

☐ I would like to work in a factory.

☐ I would like a job that involves both indoor and outdoor work.

☐ I would like to work in a science lab or hospital.

☐ I would like to work in a retail store.

☐ I would like to work in a restaurant.

☐ I would like to work on a construction site.

☐ I would like to work on a ship, plane, train, or bus.

☐ I would like to work in a hotel or resort.

☐ I would like to work in a museum or art gallery.

☐ I would like to work in an art or photography studio.

☐ I would like to work in a concert hall or theater.

☐ I would like to work in a school or library.

☐ I would like to work in a church, synagogue, temple, or mosque.

☐ I would like to work on the set of a movie or TV show.

☐ I would like to work in a TV, radio, or recording studio.

☐ I would like to work in _____ .

Working Conditions

Working conditions involve such things as what you like to work with and how you like to do your job. Consider your personality when you look at this list. Under what conditions do you feel most confident and at ease? What kinds of situations give you the most pleasure? How much structure do you like in your day? Do you like to be around people a lot, or are you just as happy being alone? Do you like to meet new people, or are you more comfortable sticking with the same circle of friends and acquaintances? Check the statements below that appeal to you.

☐ I would like a job that requires me to "dress for success" (dress up for a professional office).

☐ I would like a job that requires me to wear a uniform or costume.

☐ I would like a job that lets me dress any way I want.

☐ I would like a job that lets me work alone most of the time.

☐ I would like a job that lets me work with the same group of people.

☐ I would like a job that lets me work with many different clients.

☐ I would like a job that lets me work with ideas.

☐ I would like a job that lets me work with information.

☐ I would like a job that lets me work with computers.

☐ I would like a job that lets me work with numbers.

☐ I would like a job that lets me work with machines.

☐ I would like a job that lets me work with tools.

☐ I would like a job that lets me be creative.

☐ I would like a job that involves physical labor or activity.

☐ I would like a job with prescribed duties and procedures.

☐ I would like a job with strict deadlines.

☐ I would like a job with structured working hours.

☐ I would like a job with somewhat flexible hours.

☐ I would like a job that lets me structure my time any way I want.

☐ I would like a job that often calls for putting in extra hours.

☐ I wouldn't mind working nights or weekends.

☐ I would like a job that involves risk or danger.

☐ I would like a job that might take away my privacy.

☐ I would like a job that is intellectually challenging.

☐ I would like a job I could forget about when I'm not there.

☐ I would like to be able to work part-time when my children are young.

☐ I would like a job that involves a variety of tasks and duties.

☐ Other _____

Relationships at Work

For many people, the social aspect of a job is one of its most important parts. Advances in technology and high-speed Internet connections provide new opportunities to work from remote locations, connected to co-workers by computer. This would never work for some because of the isolation. What about you? How much social contact do you expect? Would you rather be the boss or employee? Would you like to work with specific types of people? Check the statements below that appeal to you. (Remember, telecommuters still work with people—by email, phone, fax, and occasionally face-to-face.)

- ☐ I would like to work alone.
- ☐ I would like to work in a group or on a team.
- ☐ I would like to work with a variety of people.
- ☐ I would like to be the boss.
- ☐ I would like to be supervised by others.
- ☐ I would like to work for myself.
- ☐ I would like to work with adults.
- ☐ I would like to work with children.
- ☐ I would like to work with people fighting an illness.
- ☐ I would like to work with people with disabilities.
- ☐ I would like to work with older people.
- ☐ I would like to work with creative people.
- ☐ I would like to work with people like me.
- ☐ I would like to work with people different from me.
- ☐ I would like to work with people who speak a different language.
- ☐ I would like to work with people from underprivileged backgrounds.
- ☐ I would like to teach people.
- ☐ I would like to entertain people.
- ☐ I would like to make people feel better.
- ☐ I would like to make people look better.
- ☐ I would like to help people get out of trouble.
- ☐ I would like to sell things to people.
- ☐ I would like to work with people who are incarcerated.
- ☐ I would like to give people guidance.
- ☐ I would like to run for elected office.
- ☐ I would expect to socialize with my co-workers.
- ☐ I would like to meet celebrities on my job.
- ☐ I would like to work in a competitive environment.
- ☐ I would like a job where everyone works together for the common good.
- ☐ I would like to serve the public.
- ☐ I would like to serve private clients.
- ☐ Other _____

Psychological Rewards of Working

The psychological rewards of working relate to your passions and your values. For many people, these mean much more than financial gain. Can you imagine that Mother Teresa would have given up her work with the poor to become Donald Trump's next apprentice? Did Martin Luther King, Jr., ever wish he'd gone into real estate? Did LeBron James ever consider becoming an accountant? Would Jordin Sparks enjoy a life as a computer programmer? Probably not. What do you expect to get from your job besides money? Check the statements below that appeal to you.

☐ I would like to be recognized in the community for the work I do.

☐ I would like a job where I am free to make my own decisions.

☐ I would like a job that furthers my mission in life.

☐ I would like a job that helps less fortunate members of the community.

☐ I would like a job that offers thrills and adventure.

☐ I would like a job that lets me put my family duties first.

☐ I would like a job in which I am continually learning something new.

☐ I would like a job that has high status in the community.

☐ I want to work with people I admire and respect.

☐ I would like a job that demands creativity and innovation.

☐ I would like to work for something I believe in, even if it is unpopular or puts me in danger.

☐ I would like a job that adds to the beauty in the world.

☐ I would like a job that adds to the safety of the world.

☐ I would like a position of power.

☐ I would like a job that gives me a lot of freedom.

☐ I want to feel secure that my job will be there as long as I want it.

☐ I would like to be applauded for my work.

☐ Other _____

Mixing Career and Family

While you are making career decisions, it is important to think about the kind of family life you want to have. Jobs that demand a great deal of travel or many evening and weekend hours in the office are usually not compatible with a close family life. On the other hand, if you want to have seven children, you need to think about careers that will financially support a family of that size. Today, both men and women have to be concerned about blending their career and family needs. Most women now work for pay, even when their children are very young. As a result, men need to be more involved with child care and household tasks. Since about half of all marriages end in divorce, also keep in mind that you cannot depend on the financial support of a spouse. Women, especially (86 percent of single parents are women), should prepare for careers with incomes that could support their families. Check the statements below that appeal to you.

- ☐ I want to be married.
- ☐ I want to have children.
- ☐ Family life is more important to me than my career.
- ☐ My career is more important to me than having a family.
- ☐ I would like both a rewarding career and a happy family life.
- ☐ I would like to stay home with my children when they are young.
- ☐ I would like my spouse to stay home with the children when they are young.
- ☐ I would like to work out of my house when my children are young.
- ☐ I would like a job with flexible hours so I can be available for my family.
- ☐ I would like to be able to afford to send my children to a daycare preschool.
- ☐ I would like to be able to afford to have a sitter come to the house.
- ☐ I would like to be able to afford to have live-in help with the children.
- ☐ I would like to be able to afford to have a housekeeper so I can spend more time with my family.
- ☐ I would expect my family to help out with household chores.
- ☐ Other _____

Financial Rewards

Financial rewards include not just *how much* money you make, but how you are paid, your benefits, job security, and so on. Check the statements below that appeal to you.

☐ I would like a job that pays at least $_____ per month. See page 93.

☐ I would like to be paid by the hour, with time and a half for overtime.

☐ I would like a monthly salary that doesn't vary with the number of hours I work.

☐ I would like to work on a commission basis.

☐ I would like a job that would be secure even in times of recession.

☐ I'm willing to accept a lower salary if the potential for either financial or psychological rewards is good.

☐ Money isn't important to me—I just need enough to get by.

☐ I want a job with good benefits (e.g., health insurance, pension plan, paid vacations, etc.).

☐ I'd like my salary to be based on my job performance.

☐ I'd like a job with scheduled pay increases.

☐ I'd like to be paid for the things I create or produce (e.g., paintings, articles, cookies, etc.).

☐ I'd like a job that offers bonuses or other incentives.

☐ I'm willing to start with a very low salary as long as there is an opportunity to work towards a very high salary.

☐ Other _____

Job Skills

This final category should help you fill out your general career outline. What are the skills you would most like to use on your job? Check back to chapter two and record your findings below.

My physical skills include: _____ _____

_____ _____ _____

My intellectual and creative skills include: _____

_____ _____ _____

My social skills include: _____ _____

_____ _____ _____

The skills I would like to acquire are:

_____ _____ _____

_____ _____ _____

_____ _____ _____

You will need to expand this list when you come up with a specific career goal.

You probably checked a number of statements in each category. Read them all again to get a *very* broad picture of your career desires. It's unlikely that any job could meet all these requirements, so go back and choose the one or two statements from each category that mean the most to you. Circle the boxes in front of those statements. Then enter them on the next page. Keep these in mind as you begin shortening your list of possible careers.

Gena's chart looked like this:

The physical setting I want to work in is: pleasing to the eye or an art museum or gallery.

The working conditions I would most enjoy include: a job that lets me work with many different clients and that lets me be creative.

I would like my work relationships to be: with creative people. I would also like to serve the public.

The psychological reward most important to me is: I must be continually learning something new.

My goals for mixing career and family include: having both a rewarding career and a happy family life, and being able to work out of my house while my children are young.

Financially, I would like: my salary to be based on my job performance.

The skills I have or would most like to acquire include: writing, doing research, and public speaking.

My Ideal Job

The physical setting I want to work in is: _____

The working conditions I would most enjoy include: _____

_____

I would like my work relationships to be: _____

_____

The psychological reward most important to me is: _____

_____

My goals for mixing career and family include: _____

_____

Financially, I would like: _____

_____

The skills I have or would most like to acquire include: _____

_____

Do your answers support any of the career choices you had in mind? Do they rule out any of them? Do they suggest new possibilities?

Gena found that her answers both narrowed and expanded her list of potential careers. She'd been thinking seriously about a career in business, possibly because both of her parents worked for large corporations. But that kind of job probably would not provide the kind of flexibility she'd like to have when her children are young. Besides, she wasn't sure she'd meet the most creative people working in business. Some of her answers, though, opened up new avenues of thought. She had always been interested in the arts. And her writing and researching skills could be used in a job that would let her keep on learning. Perhaps she could write about the arts or work in the public relations department of an art museum? With experience like that, she thought, she might be able to stay home and do freelance writing projects during the time she was home with her children.

Job Characteristics

Another important point to remember is that workers today have many more options than they did 20 or 30 years ago. Technological advances have created hundreds of new jobs. Changes in society have brought about changes in the workplace: flexible hours, job sharing, telecommuting, and composite careers, for example, were unheard of in the not-too-distant past. And, more than ever before, people are going into business for themselves, creating their own careers and/or businesses.

Some people are enticed by these new possibilities. Others prefer to work in more traditional modes. The new ways of working will probably give you more freedom, but they usually also involve more risks and offer less security. They require a higher anxiety tolerance. Traditional jobs offer more security and are likely to be more comfortable for those with lower anxiety tolerance. Which category appeals to you? Before you choose, make sure you know what these terms mean.

CONSIDER YOUR OPTIONS

Full-time job: A job calling for 35 to 40 hours or more of work each week.

Part-time job: A job at which you work less than 35 hours per week.

Structured hours: Strictly prescribed—and probably monitored—work hours. For example, from 8 A.M. to 5 P.M., Monday through Friday. In some jobs, employers must insist that you be on the job at a particular time. For example, if you work in a store that opens at 9 A.M., your boss is not going to take your request to show up sometime between 9 and 10:30 very seriously. If you are the anchor for the 10 P.M. news, you better be at your desk when the cameras start rolling.

Flexible hours: Work hours that provide more leeway. On some jobs, for example, you might be able to work any eight hours between 7 A.M. and 7 P.M. Many jobs offer a flexible starting time, but require all workers to be on the job during the busiest hours of the day. Self-employed people can be free to set their hours any way they like.

Composite careers: Having two or three jobs at the same time. For example, many college instructors are also researchers or writers. You might be a contractor and a cabinet maker, or a lecturer and consultant. Many people combine more secure or higher-paying jobs with higher risk or lower-paying jobs. They probably get more satisfaction from the riskier career, but their other job provides more security. This is one way to "have your cake and eat it, too."

Working for salary: Being paid by the hour or the month.

Working on a freelance or commission basis: Freelancers are paid by the job. Salespeople and agents are paid commissions, usually a percentage of their sales. For example, if a real estate broker receives a commission of 6 percent, he or she would earn $6,000 for listing and selling a $100,000 condominium.

Telecommuting: This option appeals to many, because it combines the security of working for an established company with the flexibility of completing your work at home. Rather than traveling daily to a company site, you work from another location. Telecommuting also expands a person's employment opportunities; they aren't limited to finding employment in their own community. They may live in Saint George, Utah while the company they work for is based in Santa Barbara, California—or even Buenos Aires, Argentina.

Home-based business: Technology has also made it easier to start—and maintain—your own business. With a great idea or service and some basic equipment (computer with Internet connection, fax machine, printer), a one-person, home-based office can be efficient and productive. Sophisticated software programs and the power of the Internet make being your own bookkeeper, office manager, graphic artist, marketing expert, and shipper feasible for those willing to embrace the technology learning curve.

Lifetime career: Having the same job, or same kind of job, throughout your working life.

Sequential careers: Having a series of different careers throughout your working life.

Anxiety: Worry or fear about future uncertainties. Anxiety isn't all bad, however. In fact, up to a certain point, it will help you do a better job. For example, if you are anxious about tomorrow's history test, you are more likely to prepare for it and you may perform better than if you'd had no anxiety. (Why study if you're not worried?) If you are *too* anxious, however, your performance will suffer. You'll be too nervous to do a good job.

Anxiety tolerance: How well you can deal with fears and uncertainties. Some people like the feeling that "anything could happen," or are confident that they can deal with whatever problems come along. These people have high anxiety tolerance. Those with low anxiety tolerance find the worry and fear hard to deal with. It's hard to escape anxiety, however, so learning to tolerate the discomfort is important. Remember that these fears are normal. Everyone has them. Learning to act in spite of them is a mark of maturity.

On the chart below, circle one job characteristic on each line that appeals most to you.

Column 1	Column 2
Full-time	Part-time
Structured hours	Flexible hours
Employee	Employer
Salaried	Freelance, commission
Company site	Telecommuting or home-based business
Single career	Composite careers
Lifetime career	Sequential careers

Did you circle more characteristics in column 1 or in column 2? _____

Column 1 represents careers with fewer risks, higher security, and less freedom. These careers also allow for a lower level of anxiety tolerance.

Column 2 represents careers with more risks, lower security, and more freedom. Careers like these usually call for fairly high anxiety tolerance.

Do your choices feel right for you?	Yes	No	Undecided
Do you consider yourself a risk taker?	Yes	No	Undecided
Do you often worry about future events or situations?	Yes	No	Undecided

Refer to this chart as you make your career decisions and explore different job titles. Would you be more comfortable in a job offering security or one providing more freedom? While these characteristics are at opposite ends of the scale, one is not better than the other. It's entirely a matter of what feels right for you.

Employee or Employer?

Another consideration, also based on your personality, is whether you would find it more rewarding to be an *employer* or an *employee*. Employers, as they relate to the following exercise, are defined as people who own their business, whatever its size. In other words, these people are *entrepreneurs*. They usually have more freedom and control over their time. However, they may often need to take major risks, both personal and financial. Is this an option that appeals to you?

ENTREPRENEURIAL CHECKLIST

Select the answer that best describes, or comes closest to, your feelings.

Willing to risk capital:

☐ 1. As long as I feel that there is a good chance of success, I'll go for it.

☐ 2. I'm willing to invest some capital, but I always want to leave a sizable cushion, just in case.

☐ 3. I have never really felt comfortable risking money or time on things I'm not absolutely sure of.

Independence:

☐ 1. Most of all, I want to be my own boss; it's my major goal.

☐ 2. I don't mind working for other people, but I'd rather be on my own.

☐ 3. Being on my own really scares me. I'd rather have the security of being an employee, and let someone else worry about the problems.

Flexibility:

☐ 1. I adapt to change quickly and decisively.

☐ 2. I move, but it takes time and careful consideration.

☐ 3. I would rather see things stay the same; I get uptight when change occurs.

Self-confidence:

☐ 1. I am very confident in myself and know that I can handle most situations.

☐ 2. I am confident most of the time, particularly when I know the ground rules.

☐ 3. I'm not in control of my destiny; other people really control my future.

Attitude toward people:

☐ 1. I am naturally drawn to people; I like them, and they like me.

☐ 2. I find most people enjoyable, and most people are attracted to me.

☐ 3. I like things more than people and don't have many friends.

Knowledge of the particular business:

☐ 1. I know the business that I've been thinking about well and will enjoy it.

☐ 2. I'm reasonably confident I can learn the business, and it appears that I will enjoy it.

☐ 3. I am not familiar with this type of business, nor do I know whether I will enjoy it.

Ability to start from scratch:

☐ 1. I enjoy the challenge of building something from scratch on my own; I'm a self-starter.

☐ 2. If given basic guidelines, I can do a good job.

☐ 3. I really prefer to have the entire job laid out, then I'll do it well.

Commitment:

☐ 1. I have a high drive and commitment and won't stop until the project is done.

☐ 2. I seem to have a higher level of perseverance when things are going well.

☐ 3. I start many projects, but rarely find time to finish them.

Common sense:

☐ 1. I consider myself realistic and "street wise" when it comes to business.

☐ 2. Most business situations make sense, but there are areas where I feel out of step.

☐ 3. I am inexperienced and impractical in business matters.

Willingness to accept failure:

☐ 1. "Nothing ventured, nothing gained" is my motto.

☐ 2. I want to succeed, but if I fail, I will accept it.

☐ 3. I want to avoid failure, and won't take a risk if it doesn't look like a sure thing.

Health:

☐ 1. I have excellent health and feel good, both physically and mentally.

☐ 2. I get sick on occasion, but it doesn't last long.

☐ 3. I have problems with my health; illness always seems to get in my way.

Work habits:

☐ 1. I plan before I start and then work my plan; I'm well-organized.

☐ 2. I find that I'm organized most of the time; but on occasion, I do get out of control.

☐ 3. I take things as they come, and sometimes get priorities confused.

To total your score, add up all the checked numbers. A number one has the weight of one, a number two scores a two, and a three equals three. If your total score is between 12 and 16, you are a good candidate and should consider starting your own business at some time.

This checklist is for self-evaluation of your personal characteristics, to see if you will have a better-than-average chance of success as an entrepreneur. The material may touch on some tender personal areas; you'll have to be honest with yourself. Be careful to avoid self-deception; don't brush the negative under the rug.

Take enough time to evaluate the criteria and information, and try to relate some actual experiences from your past. Determine how you will handle things when it gets tough. Because, if you can count on anything, you can count on the fact that owning your own business operation is going to be tough.

This short personal appraisal is by no means an evaluation of whether you are qualified to be an entrepreneur. It is simply a way of focusing on your personal attributes, and it may help you decide on taking that major step. You may want to ask a few of your close friends or relatives to evaluate you, perhaps more objectively than you can do it for yourself.

Reprinted with permission: *How to Start, Expand and Sell a Business, a Complete Guidebook for Entrepreneurs* by James C. Comiskey.

What About Status?

As a teen in America today, you are probably well acquainted with the concept of status. It usually comes attached to a brand name, though those names may vary widely from place to place. It's often expensive. And, it's more important to some people than it is to others.

Basically, the same rules apply to the perceived status of different careers. Certain job titles, like certain brands of jeans, offer more prestige. What is considered a high-status job may vary in different groups or circles, however. For example, a philosopher might have high status in intellectual circles, but hardly any among business-oriented groups.

Sometimes higher status is assigned to people in professions that require more education: Doctors, lawyers, college professors, and so on. Sometimes it relates to the respect society bestows on groups like the clergy. The arts, too, seem to have a certain prestige. A few jobs—in the military or the diplomatic corps, for example—come with assigned ranks so there can be no mistakes about status. In fields like sales, prestige is related to what you sell. Someone in estate jewelry, for example, will have higher status than someone who sells parts from junked cars.

Interestingly, though, status does not necessarily relate to income. That junk dealer could earn much more than the jewelry salesperson—or the doctor, for that matter. Some jobs that require just a year or two of technical training offer higher pay than many careers calling for a college degree. Plumbers and electricians, for example, have a higher average salary than teachers and librarians. In other words, just like the "right" kind of shoes, status can be expensive.

That's why you need to give some thought to your own values as you consider your job choices. In itself, status is neither good nor bad. Because some people place so much importance on it, however, it is easy to confuse your own feelings with those of your friends or parents. During your teen years, especially, peer pressure is strong, and it usually attaches the most status to meeting sex-role stereotypes: Men should be strong and brave, women should be pretty and passive. Should you make choices for your future based on these pressures? No. Remember that they will begin decreasing shortly. It will become easier to be your own person. Remember, too, that your friends will not be working at your chosen career. You will.

What does status mean to you? Whose opinions matter to you most? What values does status reflect? Can you explain why, today, a rock star has more status than a teacher or a politician? Consider these questions and then, to help clarify your thoughts, indicate whether you agree or disagree with the following statements.

It is important to me to have a job with high status.

       Agree   Disagree

I am willing to invest the time it takes to train for a job with high status.

       Agree   Disagree

It is more important to me that a job has status than that it pays well.

       Agree   Disagree

I don't think I could be happy at a job that others might look down on.

       Agree   Disagree

CHAPTER SIX

Career Research

Reading about careers isn't enough

Choose a job you love, and you will never
have to work a day in your life.
—Confucius

Every calling is great when greatly pursued.
—Oliver Wendell Holmes, Jr.

Section Two:
WHAT DO I WANT?

Marta had a dream. She didn't know exactly where she was, but it was warm and far away. And it was beautiful. There were lots of people around, but everyone seemed to be doing his or her own thing. They were all wearing shorts and T-shirts, and they worked diligently with what appeared to be tiny tools or instruments. Periodically, someone would shout excitedly, and everyone else would cheer. This went on until a brilliant sunset brought on the night. Marta woke up feeling content, but puzzled. When she shared her dream with her friend, Jennifer, she said, "I wonder what it was all about. I'd like to go back there, wherever it was."

"Sounds like some kind of archaeological dig to me," Jennifer replied.

"What's that?"

"You know. It's like looking for bones or tools or any kind of remnant of past civilizations. Archaeologists go out and recover these things, and then they study them and help put together a picture of what life was like at a certain time in a certain place."

"Oh, yeah? That sounds like something I might like to do."

Now that you've considered some of the general characteristics you'd like in a job, it's time to get more specific. As you work through this chapter, you will identify several jobs that might meet your requirements and then set out to learn as much about them as you can.

Perhaps you've already thought of some careers you'd like to know more about. If not, now's the time to start. Can you, like Marta, picture an ideal job? In addition to the work itself, think about the settings and the situations it might involve. Would you find them pleasing day-in and day-out, year after year? Take some time to daydream about your future career. Shut your eyes for a few minutes and consider different possibilities. Wait until one feels right and you, too, feel content.

Career Clusters

In order to select a career you'll be happy with, you should have some knowledge of the many jobs available. There are thousands of them, and we can't list them all here. The U.S. Department of Labor makes things a little easier by organizing jobs into Career Clusters, which you'll find on the Occupational Information Network, otherwise known as O*NET Online.

The jobs in each category have certain things in common. By investigating the family groups that appeal to you most, you may come up with quite a number of possible careers. We've listed the 23 major groups along with a few jobs in each category.

Review the Career Clusters (in bold), and place a check mark in the box next to those areas that sound interesting to you.

☐ *Agriculture, Food, and Natural Resources*

Agricultural Inspectors, Animal Breeders, Commercial Fishers, Conservation Scientists, Construction and Well Drillers, Environmental Engineers, Farm Workers and Laborers, Fish and Game Wardens, Foresters, Food Scientists, Gas and Oil Drillers, Landscapers and Groundskeepers, Logging Workers, Mining Engineers, Nursery Workers, Park Naturalists, Water Treatment Plant Operators, Zoologists

☐ *Architecture and Construction*

Architects, Bricklayers and Stonemasons, Cabinetmakers, Carpenters, Crane and Tower Operators, Construction Managers, Drafters, Electricians, Energy Auditors, Glaziers, Line Installers and Repairers, Mechanic and Repairer Helpers, Meter Readers, Painters, Pipelayers, Structural Metal Workers, Surveyors

☐ *Arts, Audio/Video Technology, and Communications*

Actors, Animators and Multi-media Artists, Announcers, Art Directors, Camera Operators, Choreographers, Costume and Wardrobe Specialists, Curators, Dancers, Film and Video Editors, Fine Artists, Graphic Designers, Interior Designers, Movie Projectionists, Musicians, News Reporters, Photographers, Producers and Directors, Sound Engineering Technicians, Writers and Authors

☐ *Business, Management, and Administration*

Accountants and Auditors, Agents and Business Managers, Billing Clerks, Budget Analysts, Business Executives, Employee Training Specialists, Human Resource Managers, Management Analysts, Meeting and Convention Planners, Office Managers, Operations Research Analysts, Public Relations Specialists, Receptionists, Secretaries, Shipping and Receiving Clerks, Supply Chain Managers, Tax Preparers

☐ *Education and Training*

Adult and Vocational Education Teachers, Coaches and Scouts, College Professors, Education Administrators, Elementary and Secondary School Teachers, Fitness Trainers and Aerobics Instructors, Instructional Coordinators, Librarians, Preschool and Kindergarten Teachers, Principals, Public Health Educators, School Counselors, Special Education Teachers, Teacher Assistants, Tutors

☐ *Finance*

Actuaries, Bank Tellers, Bill and Account Collectors, Brokerage Clerks, Compliance Officers and Inspectors, Credit Checkers and Authorizers, Economists, Financial Analysts, Financial Counselors, Insurance Adjusters and Examiners, Insurance Underwriters, Loan Officers, New Accounts Clerks, Securities Salespeople, Title Examiners and Searchers

☐ *Government and Public Administration*

City and Regional Planning Aides, Climate Change Analysts, Command and Control Center Officers, Court Clerks, Detectives and Criminal Investigators, Equal Opportunity Representatives, Government Programs Eligibility Interviewers, Government Property Inspectors and Investigators, Infantry Officers, Legislators, Municipal Clerks, Postal Service Mail Carriers, Radar and Sonar Technicians, Tax Examiners, Transportation Inspectors, Urban and Regional Planners

☐ *Health Science*

Anesthesiologists, Athletic Trainers, Biomedical Engineers, Chiropractors, Dentists, Dieticians, Emergency Medical Technicians, Family and General Practitioners, Forensic Science Technicians, Health Services Administrators, Massage Therapists, Medical Laboratory Technicians, Optometrists, Pharmacists, Psychiatrists, Registered Nurses, Speech Pathologists and Audiologists, Surgeons, Veterinarians

continued . . .

☐ **Hospitality and Tourism**

Baggage Porters and Bellhops, Bartenders, Buspersons, Casino Gaming Workers, Chefs and Cooks, Concierges, Dishwashers, Food Preparation Workers, Hotel Desk Clerks, Janitors and Housekeepers, Reservation and Ticket Agents, Restaurant Hosts and Hostesses, Tour Guides, Travel Agents, Umpires and Referees, Waiters and Waitresses

☐ **Human Services**

Child Care Workers, Clergy, Funeral Directors, Hairstylists and Cosmetologists, Laundry and Dry-Cleaning Workers, Manicurists and Pedicurists, Mental Health Counselors, Personal and Home Care Aides, Physical Therapists, Residential Advisors, Skin Care Specialists, Social and Community Service Managers, Social Workers, Sociologists, Tailors

☐ **Information Technology**

Business Intelligence Analysts, Computer Engineers, Computer Programmers, Computer Security Specialists, Computer Support Specialists, Computer Systems Analysts, Data Communications Analysts, Database Administrators, Information Technology Project Managers, Network and Computer Systems Administrators, Software Quality Assurance Engineers and Testers, Telecommunications Specialists, Video Game Designers, Web Developers

☐ **Law, Public Safety, Corrections and Security**

Animal Control Workers, Arbitrators and Mediators, Bailiffs, Corrections Officers, Crossing Guards, Dispatchers, Fire Fighters, Judges and Hearing Officers, Lawyers, Paralegals, Life Guards and Ski Patrollers, Police Patrol Officers, Probation Officers, Security Guards, Sheriffs

☐ **Manufacturing**

Appliance Installers and Repairers, Buyers and Purchasing Agents, Electric Motor Repairers, Forklift Operators, Furniture Finishers, Glass Blowers, Industrial Designers, Industrial Production Managers, Jewelers, Machinists, Packers and Packagers, Precision Assemblers, Quality Control Inspectors, Welders and Solderers, Woodworking Machine Operators

☐ **Marketing, Sales, and Service**

Advertising Managers, Cashiers, Counter and Rental Clerks, Customer Service Representatives, Floral Designers, Merchandise Displayers and Window Trimmers, Market Research Analysts, Models, Online Merchants, Real Estate Agents and Brokers, Retail Salespeople, Sales Representatives, Service Station Attendants, Stock Clerks, Wholesale and Retail Buyers

☐ **Science, Technology, Engineering, and Mathematics**

Aerospace Engineers, Anthropologists, Archaeologists, Astronomers, Biologists, Chemists, Civil Engineers, Electrical and Electronics Drafters, Engineering Managers, Energy Engineers, Hydrologists, Mapping Technicians, Meteorologists, Mechanical Engineers, Science Technicians, Statisticians

☐ **Transportation, Distribution, and Logistics**

Air Traffic Controllers, Airline Pilots, Ambulance Drivers, Automobile Mechanics, Bus Drivers, Crane Operators, Deckhands, Flight Attendants, Freight Inspectors, Locomotive Engineers, Parking Lot Attendants, Sailors, Taxi Drivers, Traffic Technicians, Transportation Security Agents, Truck Drivers

Which two groups sound the most appealing to you? Write them below.

_____   _____

Organizing occupations in career clusters is just one way of classifying different types of jobs. As you browse the Internet or look through your library's career section, you'll find others. You'll also find web sites and books about careers in specific fields, such as finance, high-tech careers, jobs of the future, careers in the arts, and so on.

You'll want to go to O*NET Online's Code Connector.* Linked to major occupational groups they call Job Families, you'll find comprehensive lists of careers within each category. This will help you develop a broad picture of careers you might find exciting and satisfying.

* At the time of this printing, the web address was http://www.onetcodeconnector.org

Bring In Your Identity

The occupational groups known as career clusters are based on broad industries with commonalities such as interests, values, and skill sets. Turn back to your personal profile chart on page 27 to review your values and passions. Now go over the groups again. Below, list a couple of careers that appeal to you most, or that seem to complement your values and passions.

_____   _____   _____

_____   _____   _____

Next take another look at your strengths and skills. Do you see (or can you think of) any careers within your chosen interest group(s) that also seem to fit in with these aspects of your personality? List other possible careers on the following lines.

_____   _____   _____

_____   _____   _____

What about your lifestyle budget? (See page 94.) That's an important piece to this puzzle. Don't forget the characteristics of your ideal job on page 134 and 137. You'll want to take your financial requirements and ideal working conditions into consideration as you proceed to the next step—in-depth research regarding specific careers and job titles.

When Letitia looked back at her bull's eye chart, she saw that her highest values were power, helping others, and personal integrity and moral courage. Looking again at her list of passions, politics, and social justice seemed to be the ones that she most wanted to be a part of her career. As she reviewed at the occupational groups, she decided that Community and Social Services and Legal were most appropriate for her.

Letitia scored high in both the dominating and influencing areas on her personal strengths test. Writing, researching, and persuading are among her skills. Therefore, she decided that becoming a lawyer was a wise choice for her. Two other careers she hadn't thought about also looked appealing— counseling and government administration. Letitia added them to her list of jobs on which to do more research.

Career Research

"Tell me and I forget. Show me and I remember. Involve me and I understand."

This sage advice should guide your career research process as you include all three steps.

Career research begins with a library investigation or an Internet search. While this is an essential part of your project, too many people make a career choice after completing this first step. Stopping your research at this point is a little like marrying someone you've been told about, but have only just met. The information you gather will not be truly meaningful until you combine it with observation and experience.

Choosing a career (like choosing a marriage partner) is one of the most important decisions you will ever make. If you take the time and energy necessary to do this job right by completing all three steps in the process, you're bound to have a happier more fulfilling life.

Remember that the choices you are making now are tentative. You may change your mind many times before settling on your future course. The career choice you make now is meant to be used for the rest of the book, not necessarily for the rest of your life. The process you are learning, however, can be useful over a lifetime, no matter how many career changes you make.

STEP ONE

READ AND RESEARCH
LIBRARY RESEARCH

You may find it useful to first visit your school or community library or Career Information Center. Most of the information you will need can be located there. Look for books in the career category or interest areas you find most interesting (agriculture, science, business, and so on).

Stop by the reference desk of your library and take a look at the U.S. Department of Labor's *Occupational Outlook Handbook* (OOH). It's revised every two years, so you'll have up-to-date information about the job: what workers do on the job, working conditions, the training and education needed, earnings, and expected job prospects.

If you haven't already done so, now is the time in your *process* to go online. The career research tools available on the Internet far exceed those found in traditional print resources. At this point in your decision-making process you've discovered your unique traits and dreams, qualities that only you can determine. Using these personal insights as a guide, start mining government databases dedicated to helping you sort through the hundreds of career opportunities available. You'll use this information to help you complete the *Career Interest Surveys* on pages 150 to 156.

CareerChoices.com

ONLINE RESEARCH

Start your Internet research with America's Career InfoNet (http://www.acinet.org). You'll find a collection of electronic tools offering unique solutions to what can be an overwhelming task. The most extensive career library online, this powerful resource will help you determine occupational requirements, identify wage and employment trends, and discover the skills required for your selected careers. You'll find information on the general job market outlook for different education levels, state-by-state labor market statistics, and short video profiles of nearly 550 jobs. Pour yourself a tall glass of your favorite beverage, turn off your cell phone, ask friends and family not to interrupt you—and search away.

Once you've found a list of career titles that intrigue you, visit the online version of the *Occupational Outlook Handbook* (OOH)* found on the Bureau of Labor Statistics' web site. Look up the job titles on your list and you'll get extensive descriptions on each. The OOH information might also include links to industry associations related to that career that you can use to expand your research.

You'll find information on employment and wage estimates for over 800 occupations on the Occupational Employment Statistics (OES).** You'll also find O*NET Online*** helpful when searching for occupations that utilize your particular skills, as discussed on pages 145 and 146.

Many magazines and newspapers archive articles on their web sites. A keyword search on any Internet search engine will uncover specialized information. Just remember, articles may become quickly outdated, so don't bother looking for information that was published more than a year or two ago.

It's also helpful to check your local newspaper's online classified ads. If remaining in your town or city is important, this is a critical consideration. You'll get a feeling for the quantity and kinds of jobs currently available in your area. To expand your search to other areas, browse the listings on web sites such as Monster.com, CareerBuilder.com, or Indeed.com.

CARL'S STORY

Carl spent a great deal of time thinking about what he wanted to do, but he was still uncertain. One day he went to a bookstore and began reading his way to his future. He went from section to section—travel, psychology, architecture—paging through books to see how he felt, what held his interest, what he wanted to know more about. When he reached the business section, he started to feel at home. He was fascinated by everything he read, and he wanted to know much more. Based on this excursion, Carl investigated business careers more seriously. His interest held. Today, he is a successful and satisfied owner of a securities brokerage house.

* At the time of this printing, the web address was http://www.bls.gov/oco
** At the time of this printing, the web address was http://stats.bls.gov/oes
*** At the time of this printing, the web address was http://www.onetonline.org/

Career Interest Survey

Now it's time to choose three careers that appeal to you most so you can begin learning as much about them as you can. Review the careers chosen on page 147. It will be helpful if you can interview people working in these fields. Separate worksheets are provided for each job.

JOB TITLE _____

1. What specific tasks would I perform on this job? (For example, a salesclerk would answer questions, tidy displays, unpack merchandise, ring up sales, make change, and so on.)

   _____

   _____

2. What is the job environment likely to be? Is this compatible with the setting I said I wanted on *page 126?*

   _____

   _____

3. What would be the rewards of working at this job? Are they the same as the ones I listed on *page 129?*

   _____

   _____

4. I would find this job particularly satisfying because: (Review your passions, values, interests, and life goals for guidance.) *See page 27.*

   _____

   _____

5. Is this job compatible with my work behavioral style? If so, in what ways? *Review pages 38–43.*

   _____

   _____

6. How much training or education would I need? Review your options (college, technical school, apprenticeship, work experience, etc.). *See pages 268–269.* What commitment am I willing to make? *Review pages 114–120.*

   _____

   _____

7. Does this job require specific physical attributes or abilities (strength or health requirements, 20/20 vision, and so on)? If so, what are they? Do I meet them?

   _____

   _____

8. What could I expect to earn as a beginner in this field? _____

   What is the average mid-career salary? _____

9. Does this meet my salary requirements? *See pages 93 and 131.*   Yes   No

   _____

10. Will there be many job openings when I am ready to go to work? How might societal,
    economic, and technological changes impact this career? *Online resources will be helpful.*

    _____

    _____

11. What aptitudes, strengths, and skills does this job call for? Are they transferable to another
    career if I change my mind or this job title becomes obsolete? *See page 132.*

    _____

    _____

12. What can I do today to begin preparing for this job?

    _____

    _____

13. What classes must I take in high school to qualify for this job?

    _____

    _____

14. Where in this town or state could I find a job in this field?

    _____

    _____

15. How does this career mesh with my family plans? Is it consistent with my desired lifestyle?
    See page 130. Does it offer opportunities for flexible hours or part-time work? Is the
    income high enough so I could maintain my family on it alone if necessary? Could I
    afford the kind of day care I'd like for my children?

    _____

    _____

    _____

16. Are there opportunities for self-employment in this field (business owner, freelance work,
    consulting, and the like)?

    _____

    _____

    _____

Create a timeline outlining how this career has changed over the last 10 years and predicting
how it might change in the next 10 years. *Start with online resources.*

My
10yearPlan
.com

JOB TITLE _____

1. What specific tasks would I perform on this job? (For example, a salesclerk would answer questions, tidy displays, unpack merchandise, ring up sales, make change, and so on.)

_____

_____

2. What is the job environment likely to be? Is this compatible with the setting I said I wanted on *page 126?*

_____

_____

3. What would be the rewards of working at this job? Are they the same as the ones I listed on *page 129?*

_____

_____

4. I would find this job particularly satisfying because: (Review your passions, values, interests, and life goals for guidance.) *See page 27.*

_____

_____

5. Is this job compatible with my work behavioral style? If so, in what ways? *Review pages 38–43.*

_____

_____

6. How much training or education would I need? Review your options (college, technical school, apprenticeship, work experience, etc.). *See pages 268–269.* What commitment am I willing to make? *Review pages 114–120.*

_____

_____

7. Does this job require specific physical attributes or abilities (strength or health requirements, 20/20 vision, and so on)? If so, what are they? Do I meet them?

_____

_____

8. What could I expect to earn as a beginner in this field? _____

   What is the average mid-career salary? _____

9. Does this meet my salary requirements? *See pages 93 and 131.*   Yes   No

_____

10. Will there be many job openings when I am ready to go to work? How might societal, economic, and technological changes impact this career? *Online resources will be helpful.*

_____

_____

11. What aptitudes, strengths, and skills does this job call for? Are they transferable to another career if I change my mind or this job title becomes obsolete? *See page 132.*

_____

_____

12. What can I do today to begin preparing for this job?

_____

_____

13. What classes must I take in high school to qualify for this job?

_____

_____

14. Where in this town or state could I find a job in this field?

_____

_____

15. How does this career mesh with my family plans? Is it consistent with my desired lifestyle? *See page 130.* Does it offer opportunities for flexible hours or part-time work? Is the income high enough so I could maintain my family on it alone if necessary? Could I afford the kind of day care I'd like for my children?

_____

_____

_____

16. Are there opportunities for self-employment in this field (business owner, freelance work, consulting, and the like)?

_____

_____

Create a timeline outlining how this career has changed over the last 10 years and predicting how it might change in the next 10 years. *Start with online resources.*

JOB TITLE _____

1. What specific tasks would I perform on this job? (For example, a salesclerk would answer questions, tidy displays, unpack merchandise, ring up sales, make change, and so on.)

_____

_____

2. What is the job environment likely to be? Is this compatible with the setting I said I wanted on *page 126?*

_____

_____

3. What would be the rewards of working at this job? Are they the same as the ones I listed on *page 129?*

_____

_____

4. I would find this job particularly satisfying because: (Review your passions, values, interests, and life goals for guidance.) *See page 27.*

_____

_____

5. Is this job compatible with my work behavioral style? If so, in what ways? *Review pages 38–43.*

_____

_____

6. How much training or education would I need? Review your options (college, technical school, apprenticeship, work experience, etc.). *See pages 268–269.* What commitment am I willing to make? *Review pages 114–120.*

_____

_____

7. Does this job require specific physical attributes or abilities (strength or health requirements, 20/20 vision, and so on)? If so, what are they? Do I meet them?

_____

_____

8. What could I expect to earn as a beginner in this field? _____

   What is the average mid-career salary? _____

9. Does this meet my salary requirements? *See pages 93 and 131.*   Yes   No

_____

10. Will there be many job openings when I am ready to go to work? How might societal, economic, and technological changes impact this career? *Online resources will be helpful.*

_____

_____

11. What aptitudes, strengths, and skills does this job call for? Are they transferable to another career if I change my mind or this job title becomes obsolete? *See page 132.*

_____

_____

12. What can I do today to begin preparing for this job?

_____

_____

13. What classes must I take in high school to qualify for this job?

_____

_____

14. Where in this town or state could I find a job in this field?

_____

_____

15. How does this career mesh with my family plans? Is it consistent with my desired lifestyle? *See page 130.* Does it offer opportunities for flexible hours or part-time work? Is the income high enough so I could maintain my family on it alone if necessary? Could I afford the kind of day care I'd like for my children?

_____

_____

_____

16. Are there opportunities for self-employment in this field (business owner, freelance work, consulting, and the like)?

_____

_____

Create a timeline outlining how this career has changed over the last 10 years and predicting how it might change in the next 10 years. *Start with online resources.*

STEP TWO

SHOW ME AND I REMEMBER

The popularity of how-to videos is evidence that this statement is true. Books about exercise, cooking, or playing tennis are often less expensive and provide more information than videos do. But somehow seeing Roger Federer hit a perfect serve or *Top Chef* contestants whip up a chicken potpie makes a more lasting impression.

As you completed your three *Career Interest Surveys,* one of your choices probably emerged as the favorite. If two or more of the jobs still hold strong appeal for you, choose the one you are least familiar with for this part of your research. If you discovered that none of the careers you investigated meet your requirements, make some new choices and go through the research and survey process once more. Again, remember that this is a tentative decision, a trial choice. Don't feel you are obligated to stick with this career simply because you are choosing it now.

When you have completed your survey and interviewed someone now working in the field of your choice, you are ready to begin step two.

SEEING IN THE MIND'S EYE

Picture yourself on the job. What would a typical working day be like? Use the information you gathered in step one to answer the following questions. Sit down, close your eyes, and actually see yourself going through the day. Pay particular attention to your feelings. Concern yourself with more than just the work. How would you feel in the morning, as you got ready to leave home? What would you do at lunch? How would you feel at the end of the day? How would you spend your evening?

IMAGING A TYPICAL DAY

If your working hours would be something other than 9:00 A.M. to 5:00 P.M., adjust the following schedule accordingly.

7:00 A.M. Getting ready for work. What would you wear? How do you feel about going to work? Are you looking forward to the day? _____

_____

8:00 A.M. Traveling to work. How would you get there? How far would you travel? Would you work at home? _____

_____

9:00 A.M. Walking into work. Describe the setting. Who else is there? What kind of greeting do you get from them? _____

_____

9:00 A.M. to 12:00 noon What would you be doing during this time? If this is a typical day, what tasks and responsibilities would you carry out?

_____

10:00 A.M. _____

11:00 A.M. _____

Noon. Where would you have lunch, and with whom? Would you socialize with co-workers? Clients?

_____

_____

1:00 P.M. to 5:00 P.M. As the day goes on, see yourself handling some special problems or challenges that might arise in this field. What are they? How do you deal with them?

_____

1:00 P.M. _____

2:00 P.M. _____

3:00 P.M. _____

4:00 P.M. _____

5:00 P.M. _____

6:00 P.M. Going home. How do you feel at the end of the day? What might you be thinking about? _____

_____

7:00 P.M. and on. How would you spend a typical evening? Would you need to bring work home? Would you be with your family? Your friends? Are there hobbies or volunteer activities you would want to pursue?

_____

_____

The Shadow Program

How difficult was it for you to see yourself on the job? Chances are, despite all your research, some of the questions were hard to answer. This exercise is meant to help you get the kind of information not likely to be found in books.

The shadow program actually lets you spend a day watching someone perform the job you want to have. First, of course, you have to get that person's permission. Write a business letter to the person of your choice, explaining what you want to do: You want to follow this person around for a day. You want to stand in the back of the room. You do not want to get in the way. You do not expect this person to spend much time with you or answer your questions during work hours. You would, however, like to have some time at lunch or after work to ask questions about the things you've seen. (Be sure to bring a notebook and pen so you can record your impressions and jot down any questions that occur to you during the day.)

Your letter should be neatly typed — and checked carefully for errors. Keep it short and to the point, but be sure to state why it is important to you to observe someone doing this job. State that you will call on a given day to get the person's response and set up an appointment if he or she is willing to take part in this program. And, be sure to say thank you.

IMPORTANT NOTE: Don't forget to send a handwritten thank you note soon after your day as a shadow.

Your letter might look something like the one below.

1426 Washington Street
Kansas City, MO 64113
April 6, 2012

Ms. Roberta Ekholm
ABC Advertising
1100 Walnut Drive
Kansas City, MO 64104

Dear Ms. Ekholm:

I am a student at Braddock School and, I hope, a future advertising copywriter. Would you be willing to let me spend a day as your "shadow" so I can learn more about what this work entails?

As your shadow, I would remain quietly in the background as you go about your daily tasks. I know that you are a busy person, and I would not expect you to take time out from your usual schedule. I would, however, appreciate it if you could take half an hour to answer my questions at the end of the day.

Although I've done thorough research on copywriting, I feel a day on the job — even in the background — would tell me so much more than I can learn from books. I will call you on Monday, April 15, to get your response. If you are willing to help me, perhaps we can schedule a day that would be convenient for you to have me around.

Thank you for your time and consideration.

Yours truly,

Pat Garibaldi

Pat Garibaldi
(123) 456-6789
Gar6789@gmail.com
patgar.blogspot.com

STEP THREE

INVOLVE ME AND I UNDERSTAND

One of the best ways to decide whether or not your career choice is a good one is to get a job in that field. You won't actually be working at your dream job, of course. But, by putting yourself in a position to watch other people do that kind of work, you can get an accurate picture of what it's like.

Your goal then is to get an entry-level job that puts you in contact with people in your chosen career. Not all jobs in your chosen field will do that. For example, delivering newspapers won't tell you very much about what it's like to be a reporter, but answering phones at the newspaper office might be enlightening.

It's fairly easy to come up with entry-level jobs for some careers. Future doctors or nurses, for example, can be candy stripers at the local hospital. Future chefs or restaurateurs might be able to bus dishes at the best restaurant in town.

What if you want to be a buyer for a department store or a lawyer? If a related entry-level job doesn't come immediately to mind, take some time to think things through. Where do the people in your career field work? An office? A courthouse? A garage? What other kinds of jobs do people do in these settings? Can you do any of those jobs?

Practice your skill at recognizing entry-level jobs by thinking of possible positions for people interested in the following careers. In column A, list jobs that will expose you to the work of each career.

Example: Mechanic = gas jockey, auto parts sales or cashier

CAREER	COLUMN A PAID	COLUMN B VOLUNTEER
Attorney		
Social Worker		
Accountant		
Veterinarian		
Police Officer		
Retail Salesperson		
Classical Musician		
Politician		
Hairstylist		
Office Manager		

HINT: If all else fails, most businesses will allow you to come in for a few hours each week and run errands. Author Mindy Bingham's brother did this for a law firm while he was in high school; he owns that same law firm today.

Keep the following points in mind as you go about your entry-level job:

1. It may not be fun or interesting. Although it's hard to stick with a job that's boring—or even nasty—keep your goal in mind. Remember that you won't have to do this forever.

2. It may not pay well; it may not pay at all. The point of this job is to learn, not necessarily to earn. If you need to volunteer your services in order to get where you want to be, do so. Many charities and social service agencies in your community will have volunteer opportunities relating to specific career fields. For example, if you're interested in a law career, you may be able to volunteer for the legal aid society. In column B on the preceding page, list volunteer jobs you could do that would put you in contact with an interesting career possibility.

CRITIQUE YOUR EXPERIENCE

The more you can "experience" actual work responsibilities and settings through opportunities like simulations, shadowing, internships, and entry-level or volunteer work, the better able you'll be to analyze whether a specific occupation is an option for you. After each work encounter, you'll want to write a critique using the following questions to stimulate your thoughts.

Once you have a job in your chosen area of interest, observe what is going on around you. Pay attention to your feelings. Do you like the setting? Do you feel comfortable? Is what is happening exciting? Does the pace of the day match your personality? Is the level of responsibility comfortable or threatening? Does the work hold your interest, or could this be boring after a short time? Do you like the people you work with? How do they seem to feel about their jobs? Are they bored? Challenged? Overworked? About how many hours a week do they work? Do they take work home with them? Are they expected to take part in after-work activities (sports, entertaining clients, and the like)? Do they travel? How often and for how long?

Your answers to questions like these should tell you whether to go ahead with your career plans or if you need to make new ones. Answer them honestly, and don't feel bad if you decide to make a change. It's much easier to do so now than it will be after you've invested years in training.

For more hints to help you find your first job, see Chapter 11 or visit www.careerchoices.com.

The Chemistry Test

When the senior class at Nicholson Hall decided to hold a dance to raise money for the homeless, class officers Jacob, Coretta, George, and Joan drew lots to decide who would be in charge of what. As a result, Coretta was designated to make centerpieces, George became the treasurer, Jacob was delegated to selling tickets, and Joan was chair of the entire event.

Initially, things did not go well. Jacob sent the tickets back three times before they were printed to his satisfaction. Worse, the thought of asking people he didn't know well to buy them made him feel quite ill at ease.

Joan needed to be sure that everyone was in agreement before she made any decisions. As a result, meetings went on for hours and everyone was frustrated.

Coretta preferred to take her own course rather than follow the directions on assembling the centerpieces. Details like that just didn't interest her. None of the decorations came out looking the same, though Coretta tried to tell everyone that they were more interesting this way.

George was into creative bookkeeping. He didn't like solitary activities like this, but when he tried to keep the books while carrying on a conversation with a friend, he made a number of mistakes.

With everything in chaos, the group was about ready to cancel the dance altogether. Then they remembered what they had learned about work behavior styles and their own personal styles in class. Assessing their strengths, they found that each had a preferred behavior style:

> Coretta — dominance
>
> George — influencing
>
> Joan — steadiness
>
> Jacob — compliance

They reassigned the duties, this time choosing the person who was best suited to each job. Since Coretta liked to be in charge and make decisions, she became the chair. George, the influencer, was a natural to take over ticket sales. Joan liked working with explicit instructions so she loved being in charge of the decorations. And Jacob, as treasurer, made sure every cent was accounted for. Accuracy was extremely important to him.

As the dance committee's story shows, your work behavior style affects the way you perform—*and the way you feel about*—a job. Turn back to page 43 and review the four classic work styles. Everyone has to be able to use each of the styles to some extent, but one of them is probably the most comfortable for you. Which one?

TEAM BUILDING

Match the four people described below with the job for which his or her chemistry test would "qualify" them in each of the work environments listed. If you were in charge of the businesses, how would you assign these employees to build the most effective team?

Ellen's preferred behavior style is dominance. She is a high-energy individual who likes to be in charge of what she is doing. She is decisive and always looks for the most efficient way to do things. She likes to solve problems, is comfortable with change, and is very goal directed.

Robert's style is influencing. He is a creative person who likes flexibility in his work environment. He is gregarious and likes to work with people. Robert's enthusiasm can be contagious. He is good at persuading people to act. He likes varied tasks and will take calculated risks.

Michiko is most comfortable with steadiness. She likes to work with other people, particularly in a supportive role. A patient and considerate person, Michiko likes tasks with well-defined procedures. A steady worker, she follows her project through from beginning to end. She is a listener and a doer.

Romero's preferred style is compliance. He is extremely detail oriented and is likely to question the decisions of others. He wants to know the facts behind the issues. A conscientious worker, he is precise in any task he undertakes and wants to make sure it is done accurately.

MATCHING WORK STYLES TO JOBS

How would you assign the jobs below to these four individuals?

For example, in a book publishing company, jobs would be assigned like this:

BOOK PUBLISHING
Publisher: *Ellen*
Sales Rep: *Robert*
Book designer: *Michiko*
Editor: *Romero*

CONSTRUCTION

Draftsperson _____

Contractor _____

Architect _____

Carpenter _____

HOSPITAL

Minister/priest/rabbi _____

Administrator _____

Lab technician _____

Physician _____

FACTORY

Cafeteria chef _____

Assembly line worker _____

Foreman _____

Quality control inspector _____

SCHOOL

Secretary _____

Principal _____

Attendance clerk _____

Counselor _____

BANK

Loan officer _____

Bank teller _____

Manager _____

Accountant _____

RESEARCH LAB

Project manager _____

Fundraiser _____

Scientist _____

Computer programmer _____

Even within career categories, certain specialties may be more suited to one behavior style than to the others. Can you identify which personality type would likely be happiest in each of the jobs below? Review the definitions of behavioral style on page 43. Then, although this is not an exact science, see what makes sense to you. Be prepared to defend your choices in discussion.

WRITER

Freelance magazine writer: *dominance*

Copywriter for advertising agency: *influencing*

Reporter for local newspaper: *steadiness*

Technical writer for science textbooks: *compliance*

PHYSICIAN

Anesthesiologist _____

Surgeon _____

Chief of physicians at local hospital _____

Teacher at medical school _____

TEACHER

Teacher in public school system _____

Private tutor or coach _____

Professor of accounting at university level _____

Trainer for major corporation _____

CHEF

Head chef in a large restaurant—tastes everything! _____

Catering company owner _____

Teacher of adult education cooking classes _____

Associate chef in a restaurant _____

Answers:

Dominance: Freelance magazine writer, chief of physicians, private tutor or coach, catering company owner

> People in these jobs are all self-directed. They are in charge.

Influencing: Copywriter, teacher at medical school, trainer for major corporation, teacher of adult education cooking classes

> People in these careers work closely with others and are involved with teaching or influencing them.

Steadiness: Reporter for local newspaper, anesthesiologist, teacher in public school system, associate chef in restaurant

> These workers like a highly-defined set of procedures. They enjoy supportive, predictable roles.

Compliance: Technical writer for science textbooks, surgeon, professor of accounting at university level, head chef in large restaurant

> People in these jobs are precise and exacting and concerned about quality control.

Which career seems to be your favorite choice at this point in time? What work behavior style do you think would be prominent in someone happy with this job?

_____

Why? _____

_____

Does this match your personal work style? Review your answers on page 42.

Yes   No   Perhaps

In what ways?

_____

_____

To gain a better understanding of your own style, talk with your teacher or counselor about taking the complete DiSC *Personal Profile System*® test. By taking the complete assessment, you'll discover particulars about yourself that will help you match your traits with specific careers and tasks.

Has your research led you to a tentative career choice? If not, the next chapter offers a model you can use to help make this—or any—decision.

Information on personality styles is adapted from the widely-used DiSC™ Dimensions of Behavior model and the *Personal Profile System*® assessment instrument, ™copyright 1972, Carlson Learning Company. Used with permission of Carlson Learning Company, Minneapolis, Minnesota.

No trumpets sound when the important
decisions of our life are made. Destiny is
made known silently.
                              —Agnes De Mille

Choice, not chance, determines destiny.
                              —Anonymous

CHAPTER SEVEN

Decision Making

How to choose what's best for you

Section Two:
WHAT DO I WANT?

Lake Byron

MT Rd.

Dunk Peak

Blue River

Mt. Cooper

Sandy

Worthy Hill

O Path

10 Road

Blue Pond

Div Road

ME Road

Quint was starting his junior year of high school, and, as his parents never seemed to tire of telling him, it was time to make some decisions about his future. Quint wondered why he should bother. Everyone else seemed to know exactly what he should do.

His parents wanted Quint to attend their alma mater, a private college in another state. His football coach said that, if he attended the local junior college, Quint was sure to be a starter on the team there. And, if he did well, he might even be able to play for a four-year school after that. Ms. Watson, his math teacher, thought Quint should attend the state university, which had an excellent engineering program. His friends wanted Quint to join them on a cross-country motorcycle trip. They all needed a break from school, they said.

But what did he want? Quint wasn't sure, and he didn't really like to think about it. He wished the whole subject would just go away.

Thad Path

Violet Lake

Golden Path

Laker Road

Ermine Meadow

Making decisions can be difficult for a young adult. You grow up learning to please your parents or your teachers. Then, suddenly, you're supposed to know how to please yourself. When did *that* become the issue?

Actually, it's always been the issue, and you are probably better at making decisions than you realize. When, for example, was the last time you took your parents' advice on what TV show to watch or what to wear to school?

Because making these decisions is so easy, you may not be aware of the process behind them. Using it is almost automatic. But, by becoming *aware* of the steps involved, you can apply this process to decisions in almost every area of your life.

Let's take apart one of these easy decisions—what to wear to school, for example. The first thing you probably do is think about your image or what you would like your image to be. Your goal, then, is to dress in a way that will enhance this image. The logical next step is to consider your choices—the clothes you have or your budget for buying anything new. You can immediately rule out certain items, like the shirt Aunt Grace sent you from her last vacation, which, apparently, was to the planet Mars, and the boots you were wearing when you decided to walk through the cow pasture at night.

Before you make your decision, you will also probably think about what *other people* wear—especially the people who fit your goal image. Finally, you evaluate your choices and consider which of your outfits comes closest to meeting your goal. And that's your decision.

Some decisions are harder to make, but the process is the same. On the following pages, you will learn a decision-making model that, with practice, can become as automatic as getting dressed in the morning.

Identifying Choices

Joyce decided she wanted to be a doctor the day her little sister was hit by a car. She saw how the staff at the emergency room calmly went about saving Sheila's life, as though they did this sort of thing every day. "Of course," Joyce thought later, "they do!" She couldn't imagine a more wonderful job.

She also wants to buy a car. There's no room for this in the family budget, so Joyce needs to come up with the money on her own. She could get a job at the local fast food restaurant (it's about the only employer for teens in her town), but she worries about the effect on her grades. If they fall, she won't be able to get into the college she wants to attend. She also thinks that it might be a good idea to volunteer at the hospital in order to get some experience, but she clearly can't do this and hold down a paying job as well.

List Joyce's goals below.

1. _____

2. _____

Which would you say is her long-term goal? Which is her short-term goal?

It's important to differentiate between the two. Short-term goals are those things that seem essential to your happiness *right now.* Because achieving them can result in immediate gratification, it's tempting to focus on them. Long-term goals, after all, might take *years* to fulfill. Shouldn't you be allowed some happiness in the meantime?

Of course you should, and you will have happiness. But, make sure it's not at the expense of your future. In 10 years, what will mean more to you—an impressive wardrobe or a rewarding career? An aging car or a comfortable income? If you consider your long-term goals first, decision making will become much easier.

What is Joyce's long-term goal? _____

What are the options she must choose from now that will effect her long-term goal?

1. _____

2. _____

3. _____

Gathering Information

Once you've determined what your choices are, you need to find out as much as you can about each option in order to make an informed decision. This is a term that usually refers to a decision based on facts and/or thought. The more information you have about your choices, the better your decision is likely to be.

Before Joyce decides to take a job in the fast-food restaurant, for example, she needs to find out:

1. How much the job would pay per hour
2. How many hours a week she could work
3. What the down payment and monthly payments would be on the kind of car she wants to buy
4. How much she would need to spend each month on insurance, maintenance, and gas for the car

Without this information, Joyce might decide to take the job only to find that she still can't afford to buy a car. Considering that she may have jeopardized her future by taking time away from her studies, this would have been a bad decision for Joyce.

Take another look at Joyce's choices:

1. To take a job in a fast food restaurant
2. To volunteer at the hospital
3. To spend her time studying and maintaining her grades

Before she can choose the best alternative, she needs to know:

1. What grades she needs to get into the college of her choice
2. Which classes she must take in order to major in pre-med
3. The availability of and requirements for financial aid or scholarships at this college
4. How much she could expect to earn on the job

Can you list some other information that would be helpful to Joyce as she weighs her alternatives?

1. _____

2. _____

3. _____

4. _____

Evaluating Choices

When you've listed your alternatives and learned as much as you can about each of them, you are ready to evaluate your choices. A good way to do this is to list the pros and cons of each choice. You must also judge how likely each alternative is to be successful or get you what you want.

As you may have noticed, this process calls for a certain amount of guesswork. It is also possible to "load the deck" in favor of the choice you would like to think is most appropriate for you. It is in your best interest, however, to be as honest as you can while making your evaluations. This *is* the time, though, to consider your *feelings* about your choices. Taking into account the information you've gathered, does your intuition tell you that one course is most suitable for you now? (Many people are inclined to base decisions on their hunches *before* they've investigated the facts. If you're going to use your intuition, it's important to use it in *light of,* not *in spite of,* what you know.)

No matter how thorough and honest you are, though, it is not always clear which choice you should make. Each alternative will have its pros and cons, and there are no guarantees that any course you take will be successful. By keeping your goals and values firmly in mind, however, you can be confident of making good decisions most of the time.

Joyce began evaluating her choices on the chart below.

In the spaces remaining on the chart, evaluate Joyce's other choice—not to work at all so she can concentrate on her studies.

Identify your choices	Evaluate your choices		
	Pros	Cons	Probability of success
Working at fast food restaurant	Earn money to buy car	Not related to medicine —therefore no relevant experience	Since I am smart and reliable, I should be able to get this job
Volunteer at the hospital	First medical job for resume	Less study time —may lower grades	Since I am smart and reliable, I should be able to get this job
Not work at all	_____	_____	_____
	_____	_____	_____

172

JESSICA'S STORY

Jessica needs to decide whether to take a math class next year and, if so, which one. She could take Algebra 2, but she knows it's hard. Getting a good grade would mean less time for socializing with friends in the evening. Basic math would be easier. She always got As and Bs in grade school math, so it should be a cinch. She could even get by with no math class at all. She doesn't like math that much, but her counselor, Ms. Briscoe, reminded her that math isn't important for what it lets you become; it's important for what it keeps you from becoming. She said that, without math, Jessica was cutting her options for future careers by 75 percent. Did she really want to do that?

Use the chart below to identify Jessica's choices and evaluate each one.

Identify your choices	Evaluate your choices		
	Pros	Cons	Probability of success
1. _____ _____	_____	_____	_____
2. _____ _____	_____	_____	_____
3. _____ _____	_____	_____	_____
4. _____ _____	_____	_____	_____

If you were Jessica, what would you do? _____

_____

_____

173

JOHN'S STORY

John is bored with school. He doesn't see how any of his classes relate to real life. Besides, he's probably going to fail English. Why not just drop out and go to work, he wonders. He's confident he could get a job in highway construction. He does enjoy the time he spends in the school's computer lab, however. The new graphic design software is especially intriguing. He's done some good work on it. He's heard of a technical school that offers a program in this field. The school counselor told John that, if he brought his grades up, he could even get a degree in this field from the local college. Or, maybe he should join the army. The recruiter promises John could get specialized training there.

Use the chart below to identify John's choices and evaluate each one.

Identify your choices	Evaluate your choices		
	Pros	Cons	Probability of success
1. _____	_____	_____	_____
_____	_____	_____	_____
2. _____	_____	_____	_____
_____	_____	_____	_____
3. _____	_____	_____	_____
_____	_____	_____	_____
4. _____	_____	_____	_____
_____	_____	_____	_____

If you were John, what would you do? _____

_____

_____

Decision-Making Model

The decision-making model you've just learned should work well in most instances. When you are making decisions about long-term goals, however, you will also want to take your resources, wants, and needs into consideration. This will let you see "the big picture" and should help motivate you to follow through with the actions that will help you achieve your goals.

The comprehensive decision-making model includes these steps:

1. **Define your goal.**
2. **State the decision to be made.**
3. **Analyze your resources.**
4. **Analyze your wants and needs.**
5. **Identify your choices.**
6. **Gather information.**
7. **Evaluate your choices.**
8. **Make your decision.**

Note: You've already done much of this work. In chapter 2, page 27, you analyzed your resources. You analyzed your wants and needs in chapters 3–5. And, in chapter 6, you identified your choices and gathered information on pages 150–155.

GLORIA'S CHART

Goal: Become a computer repair technician

Decision to be made: How and if to get the training I need

Resources: Basic knowledge of computers
Good with hands
Like working with computers
Love detail work
Love to take things apart and put things together

Wants and needs: Value security—there will always be computers to repair
Want to work for myself someday to have flexibility for raising family
Want to be able to support family on one income if necessary

Gather information: Review my *Career Interest Survey* for computer repair technician

Identify your choices	Evaluate your choices		
	Pros	Cons	Probability of success
1. Go to trade school	—certifiable training, best guarantee of a job	—costs time and money	—should have no trouble getting into this program or doing this work
2. Learn on the job	—earn while I learn, use my skills	—probably low pay during training, no certificate, therefore lower pay in the long run	—may have to compete for opening, but can probably do the work
3. Become a waitress	—no training necessary, possibly higher immediate earnings	—not what I want to do forever, little security, doesn't make use of my skills	—should be able to get a a job in this field

What choice would you make if you were Gloria? _____

_____

Gloria decided to take a two-year apprenticeship and save some of her earnings to pay for trade school and a certification.

DECISON-MAKING RUBRIC

Complete the chart below for yourself. Identify and evaluate four possible career choices.

Goal: To identify a career that I will find satisfying.

Decision to be made: Which career would I find most satisfying?

My resources: _____

_____

_____

_____

My wants and needs: _____

_____

_____

_____

Gather information: _____

Identify your choices	Evaluate your choices		
	Pros	Cons	Probability of success
1. _____ _____	_____ _____	_____ _____	_____ _____
2. _____ _____	_____ _____	_____ _____	_____ _____
3. _____ _____	_____ _____	_____ _____	_____ _____
4. _____ _____	_____ _____	_____ _____	_____ _____

Make a choice _____

How realistic is this choice? _____

My
10yearPlan
.com

Make a Decision

Making a decision is often difficult, but there's no way around it. You can stall and fret and change your mind. Sooner or later, though, *not* making a decision is making a choice. If you can't decide what to have for lunch, you are choosing not to eat. If you can't decide who to ask to the dance, you are choosing to go alone—or not to go at all. If you can't decide which college to attend, you are choosing not to attend college.

Decisions can—and often should—be changed. Many people fear making them because they think that mistakes are not permissible, that there's only one correct course of action. However, people don't make decisions simply to be right. Executives, for example, are paid to make decisions so that work can proceed. They make the best decisions they can, but sometimes the decisions need to be changed. The point is, it's necessary to take action, and that's what making a decision allows you to do.

Basically, there are two styles of decision avoidance. Some people just can't bear to think about their choices at all and they let things happen by default. This is a passive behavior pattern. The other extreme is more aggressive. People with this behavior pattern suffer from "paralysis by analysis." They insist on examining every option and collecting every bit of information. But, afraid they may have overlooked something, they never quite get around to making a decision.

What is your decision-making (or avoiding) style? Check the places along the scale below that you think best represent your personality. If the words in the left-hand column describe your behavior, you may tend to avoid making decisions. On the other hand, if your behavior is better described by the words on the right, you may tend to make decisions too quickly. There is no right or wrong spot on the scale. But, by being aware of your tendencies, you may be better able to use them in your best interest.

passive	___	___	___	___	___	___	___	aggressive
contemplative	___	___	___	___	___	___	___	impulsive
controlled	___	___	___	___	___	___	___	free
rational	___	___	___	___	___	___	___	emotional
easily influenced	___	___	___	___	___	___	___	self-directed
delaying	___	___	___	___	___	___	___	expediting
cautious	___	___	___	___	___	___	___	risk-taking
structured	___	___	___	___	___	___	___	creative
agonizing	___	___	___	___	___	___	___	relaxed

By using the decision-making model—being as honest with yourself as possible—you may not always make the best decision. But you are probably not going to make the worst one, either. Letting others make your decisions, or making them by default, is giving up control of your life and your future. This is not the way to find satisfaction.

Evaluate your options, use your best judgment, take a deep breath, and make up your mind.

Keeping Your Options Open

It may seem that you are limiting your options when you make a decision. Sometimes you are. Deciding to quit school or to have a baby at age 16 can really put a crimp in your social life and your financial future.

Since making decisions is inevitable, however, keeping your options open is one more factor to consider when you make your plans. Should you take the classes you'll need to get into college even if you're not sure you want to go? Which decision would give you the most flexibility?

Remember that few decisions are irreversible or fatal. You *can* change your mind. And the better you get at making decisions, the better you'll be able to judge when it's time to make a change.

Flexibility is an important attribute that shows every sign of being even more important in the future (more on this later). As the world changes, or as your own values, wants, and needs evolve, you will need to make adjustments—new decisions. With practice, you'll become secure in the knowledge that you've done it before and you can do it again.

You've made a decision. It's time to make your plans.

The rest of the book concerns HOW TO GET WHAT YOU WANT.

CHAPTER EIGHT

Setting Goals and Solving Problems

Skills for successful living

I always view problems as opportunities
in work clothes.

— Henry J. Kaiser

Efforts and courage are not enough
without purpose and direction.

—John F. Kennedy

Section Three:
HOW DO I GET IT?

> You can't build a reputation on what you're going to do.
> —Henry Ford

Getting what you want differs from *deciding* what you want in one very important way: *It requires action.* It's easier to fantasize your future than it is to build it, but you must build it all the same. The remaining chapters in this book will teach you some processes that should be of help. *You* will need to come up with the energy, motivation, and confidence to get your plans off the ground, however.

HUBERT'S STORY

More than anything in the world, Hubert wanted to be appointed to the U.S. Air Force Academy. His father attended the academy, and he said it was the best experience of his life. "It'll be even better for me," Hubert told himself. "I'll be a fighter pilot. I'll be a hero! Why not?" Hubert spent many hours in front of the mirror, trying his father's old hat on to see which angle was most flattering, and practicing the squint he was sure made him look like a young Johnny Depp. "Or should I go for the Orlando Bloom look?" Hubert mused.

Just one thing was standing in his way: Hubert's grades were well below the average he needed if he hoped to achieve his goal. Finding time to study seemed impossible. It was all he could do to finish reading the sports section of the newspaper before dinner. And, in the evenings, he had to hang out with his friends or maybe take a date to the movies. Plus there were all those great shows on TV. When Hubert's mother suggested he study on Saturday and Sunday afternoons, he was amazed. "Are you kidding?" he said. "During football season?"

Sometimes Hubert got discouraged. It wasn't really his fault. Could he help it if his friends wanted to go out so much or if his teachers were less than understanding about his plight? He had nothing to do with setting up the admission standards, which, if you asked him, were totally unreasonable. There was always hope, though, Hubert insisted. Maybe the requirements would be lowered next year—at least for him. Surely, when he explained, they'd see things his way. It was probably just a myth, that business about the military putting so much stock in following rules. Why worry? Everything would be fine, Hubert decided, as he flicked on the TV.

Tools For Solving Problems

Whether he admits it or not, Hubert has a problem, and the prospects of his solving it are not good. If he doesn't change his ways, Hubert's life is likely to be plagued with unsolved problems.

Yours needn't be, however. Problem solving takes time and effort. It takes self-discipline, a quality with which Hubert is not well acquainted. But, it can be done. In his book, *The Road Less Traveled,* author M. Scott Peck lists four techniques that, used together, should be helpful. Dr. Peck points out that using his techniques is not easy or painless. He says, in fact, that they will cause you a certain amount of suffering. However, the pain is temporary, and it can lead to rewards that make it seem insignificant.

The first tool or technique, according to Dr. Peck, is **delaying gratification**. This means doing without the double fudge brownie you'd like to have now for the sake of the satisfaction you'll feel next month when you've lost five pounds. For Hubert, making the effort to bring his grades up now would mean giving up time he'd like to spend with his friends or watching TV. But, if he gets into the Air Force Academy as a result, he might feel his sacrifices were worthwhile.

Delaying gratification is difficult because the rewards of living only for the moment are more tangible. You can taste that brownie. The pounds you thought you wanted to lose seem much more abstract, however. And, when temptation strikes, long-term goals can easily be forgotten or postponed.

As you learn to delay gratification—put off the temporary joys of today in favor of lasting rewards in the future—you will be acquiring an important tool in solving problems.

The second technique in Dr. Peck's problem-solving prescription is **accepting responsibility**. Hubert was willing to blame his friends, his teachers, even the TV programmers, for his bad grades. Passing the blame is not effective in solving problems. When the problem is yours, so is the responsibility to solve it.

This is a difficult fact to accept. Sometimes other people do things that upset you or disrupt your plans. If Hubert's friends didn't ask him to go out, for example, he might find it easier to get his studying done. But it is Hubert who wants to go to the Air Force Academy, and it is Hubert's responsibility to get the grades he needs to do that. His friends are his friends. They are not his keepers, counselors, or homeroom monitors. If Hubert could accept responsibility for his actions—and his problem—he would say no to his friends and struggle through his studies which, in the long run, will help him achieve his goals.

The *good* news on this point is that taking responsibility also gives you the opportunity to choose. And, just as you are responsible for becoming the person *you* want to be, you are *not* responsible for becoming the person anyone else wants you to be. Pressure from home or from friends can be intimidating. It's natural to want to please the people you care about. But, if they want you to do something you feel is not truly you or not something you want to become, you can "just say no" with a clear conscience.

Dedication to truth or reality is the third problem-solving technique you need to master. Wishful thinking has not been shown to be an effective way to solve problems. It *is* popular, however. That is why we still see ads proclaiming that you can "lose weight painlessly overnight," or "make a million dollars at home in your spare time."

As long as Hubert clings to the belief that the regulations do not apply to him, he has no motivation to try to meet them. He should remember that the admissions committee is not privy to his daydreams. They have a procedure to follow, and they will apply it to him as well as to everyone else who wants to gain admission. "The truth isn't always pretty," as they say, but you cannot solve a problem by denying it exists.

Finally, problem solving requires **balancing**, which leads to *flexibility*. According to Dr. Peck, balancing is "the type of discipline required to discipline discipline." In other words, there are times when you *shouldn't* delay gratification. It's important to know how to live joyously in the moment—as long as you aren't being self-destructive by doing so.

And, even though it is important to recognize truth or reality, it is not always appropriate to act on that truth. You may be angry with a teacher who assigns too much homework on weekends, for example. However, throwing a tantrum and stomping on your books is not going to change the situation or improve your standing in class.

In short, balancing requires judgment. Although you may be too young to always know the correct action to take in a given circumstance, you *can* learn to think things through before you act, and make an honest effort to take the most effective or least destructive course.

"I must do something" will always solve more problems than "Something must be done."
— Anonymous

Crystal and Sterling were high school sweethearts who wanted to get married right after graduation. They didn't have any money and they both wanted to go to college, but they didn't see why either of those facts should stand in the way. They were surprised and angered when Crystal's parents said the young couple would not be able to live with them, and Sterling's parents, even more unreasonably, said that if he and Crystal married, they wouldn't even pay his college tuition, as they had promised. "Alright then," said Sterling, "I guess I'll just have to get a job." Crystal, who was very good at math, quickly determined that, if Sterling earned the minimum wage (he was unlikely to find a better paying job) he would only make $15,000 a year. That was clearly not enough to support the two of them, even if she did get an athletic scholarship, as she hoped.

Who is responsible for solving Crystal and Sterling's problem?

_____

If they get married right away, what sacrifices might they have to make?

_____

_____

If they wait and get married when they graduate from college, what sacrifices will they

have to make? _____

_____

What facts should Crystal and Sterling consider before they make their decision?

_____

_____

What wishful thinking might come into play as they make their decision? How likely is

that to happen? _____

_____

If you were Sterling and Crystal, what would you do? _____

_____

Setting Goals and Objectives

Remember Marta's story, back on page 144?

After talking with her friend Jennifer, Marta decided she would like to know more about archaeology. Do archaeologists spend more of their time in the field or in the office? Who do they work for? How much education would she need? Where is most of the field work being done these days? Is it really hot there? Rainy? Would there be snakes?

These were all things she wanted to know before registering for the classes she would take next year. That gave her two months to do her research. Marta developed an action plan: She set her goal and then listed objectives for getting the information she needed.

Marta's action plan looked like this:

Goal: To answer my questions about archaeology by March 1.

Objective 1: Read at least one book or four articles on archaeology by January 20.

Objective 2: Search the Internet for information and discussion groups by January 25.

Objective 3A: Call City College and the Natural History Museum by January 31 to see if there are any archaeologists on staff.

Objective 3B: If so, interview a working archaeologist by February 14.

Objective 4: Research climate and reptile life at the three most appealing field sites by February 21.

Marta's action plan consists of setting goals and objectives. If she follows her plan, it is likely to get her the information she needs by the time she needs it.

Think of goals and objectives as a kind of recipe for getting what you want. The goal is the end product you want to achieve within a certain amount of time: Let's say chocolate chip cookies (30 minutes). The objectives are the ingredients and the methods you use to make them. Once you know what the goal is (cookies), it's relatively easy to focus on the objectives (find the semi-sweet chips, never mind the onions).

Like ingredients, objectives are measurable (2 eggs, 3 cups of flour). And, like a recipe, they give you a time-frame in which to work (bake for 12 minutes at 350 degrees).

The more specific your goals and objectives, the more helpful they will be. Consider the recipe once again. What if, instead of chocolate chip cookies, it was called "chewy, sweet things with brown parts inside"? Would you still have a pretty good idea of what you were making? Would you even be tempted to try? And, what if the recipe called for "a bunch of eggs" and "some sugar," and directed you to "bake until sometime in the future"? What are your chances of ending up with something even your little brother, the walking waste disposal, wouldn't eat?

Let's go over the definitions again, this time without the cookies.

A goal is a statement that specifies what you want to achieve or do within a certain amount of time. An objective is an action that will help you meet your goal—and measure your success. An objective tells you what will be different when you've accomplished it, by how much or how many, and by when.

Take a look at Marta's first objective:

To read at least one book or four articles on archaeology by January 20.

> **What will be different when Marta achieves this objective?** We've underlined that part of her statement.
>
> **By how much or how many?** The triangles point out the numbers.
>
> **By when?** Notice the circled date.

Using these same symbols, go back to page 186 and diagram Marta's other objectives.

Now write and diagram some objectives of your own. Choose two goals from the following list and write three objectives for each.

To buy a new car in six months.

To save for a trip to _____ after graduation.

To make the _____ team next year.

To earn an A in _____ class.

To be accepted at _____ after high school graduation.
   (school)

Goal: _____

Objectives:

1. _____

2. _____

3. _____

Goal: _____

Objectives:

1. _____

2. _____

3. _____

YOUR LIFESTYLE GOALS

Now write some goals and objectives of your own. Turn back to page 63 and choose three statements about your desired lifestyle. Write a goal and three objectives for each one. Focus on three goals you can meet in the coming year that would help you achieve a more satisfying future. Diagram the objectives to make sure they include all necessary components.

One of Maria's lifestyle goals was:

To have a career that is flexible enough to accommodate raising a family.

Her objectives:

1. Over the next two months, to interview five professional women who are successfully mixing career and family.

2. By the end of the semester, to research and identify eight careers that are flexible and yet offer the economic security required for a family.

3. By the end of the semester, to visit my counselor and make sure I am taking the necessary courses to prepare me for careers meeting my requirements.

Your lifestyle goal: _____

   Objectives:

     1. _____

     2. _____

     3. _____

Your lifestyle goal: _____

   Objectives:

     1. _____

     2. _____

     3. _____

Your lifestyle goal: _____

   Objectives:

     1. _____

     2. _____

     3. _____

New beliefs/values

New dreams

Growth or change

New goals

NEW GOALS AS WE GROW

Along with our careers, our lifestyles are determined largely by our values, opportunities, and desires—all things that tend to change over the course of a lifetime. When we set goals, we do so in an attempt to satisfy our present values. In reaching those goals, however, our minds are stretched, our limits are extended—and we change. We are constantly testing ourselves and our abilities. In the process, we often find that we have found new values and set new goals, and so the process repeats itself. As our values change, our goals change. Reaching new goals leads to recognizing new values, and so on.

Keep in mind that life is an ever-changing and ever-growing process. The most satisfied people among us are those who actively set and reach new goals throughout their lives. If you can master this process, you are likely to have a rewarding future.

Nothing in life is to be feared. It is only
to be understood.

—Marie Curie

CHAPTER NINE

Avoiding Detours and Roadblocks

The road to success is dotted with many tempting parking places

I have learned that success is to be measured not so much by the position that one has reached in life as by the obstacles which one has overcome while trying to succeed.

— Booker T. Washington

Section Three:
HOW DO I GET IT?

Many of the students at Carlos's high school were from wealthy families. Although Carlos's parents earned a comfortable living, they couldn't give him the cars or vacations his friends took for granted. They were proud when Carlos was accepted for admission at a well-known liberal arts college, but they told him he would have to help pay his own expenses. Carlos angrily told his parents that none of his friends had to do that. He wouldn't go to college at all if he had to work, too. It would be too hard. And, besides, it just wasn't fair.

No one in Liz's family had ever graduated from high school, much less gone to college. She'd always dreamed of becoming a teacher, but she decided that wasn't realistic. What made her think she was any better than her family and friends? It wouldn't be fair to leave them behind.

Karla liked to think about being a mechanical engineer, but she knew she'd never be one. She didn't know any women who were mechanical engineers. And, besides, she'd have to take all that math. It would be too hard.

Christy was one of many children in a poor family. He had cerebral palsy and didn't even begin to speak until he was 11 or 12. The only part of his body he could use was his left foot. He learned to type and paint with it, and eventually became recognized as both a writer and artist.

There are two important things you should know about life: it's not easy, and it isn't always fair.

The way you choose to respond to these facts will greatly affect your successes and life satisfaction. The first three stories are made up, but illustrate some common attitudes. The fourth story is true. Christy Brown was an Irish painter and writer. He accepted his illness as a challenge and set out to see what he could do with his life.

There are many people like Christy Brown, people whose attitudes take them far beyond what others would expect them to achieve. There are also many people like Carlos, Liz, and Karla, who let their attitudes limit their opportunities.

It's easy to find reasons to complain. It's easy to give up on a dream without trying harder to achieve it. But it's impossible to find satisfaction in a life that's based on negative feelings and behaviors.

Ironically, realizing that life is hard—for everyone—somehow makes it easier to overcome the obstacles and achieve your aspirations.

This chapter should help you recognize some of the most common detours and roadblocks to success so you can avoid them.

I Can't Do It Because…

I'd like to kiss you, but I just washed my hair.
—from an old Bette Davis movie

People can be extremely creative when thinking of excuses for not doing something. That's not surprising when the action to be avoided is undesirable. What is puzzling, though, is how often we make excuses for not doing the things we most want to do!

You may believe that your excuse is valid, but somewhere, someone with the same problem or affliction is busy living your dream. Are you just going to sit there and let that happen? Why?

The responsibility of stating who you want to be and how you are going to get there can be very frightening. However, not doing so is generally much worse and can lead to a life of considerable dissatisfaction and unhappiness.

What's Your Excuse?

Ninety-nine percent of the failures come from
people who have the habit of making excuses.
— George Washington Carver

We've listed some pretty convincing excuses below. Check any that apply to you.

- ☐ I'm a woman
- ☐ I'm a man
- ☐ I'm black
- ☐ I'm white
- ☐ I'm Hispanic
- ☐ I'm Asian
- ☐ I come from a different culture
- ☐ I'm rich
- ☐ I'm poor
- ☐ I'm too smart
- ☐ I'm not smart enough
- ☐ I'm too ugly
- ☐ I'm too fat
- ☐ I'm too thin
- ☐ I'm too short
- ☐ I'm too tall
- ☐ I'm blind
- ☐ I have impaired vision
- ☐ I'm deaf
- ☐ I have a hearing loss
- ☐ I can't speak
- ☐ I have a speech impediment
- ☐ I'm a paraplegic

- ☐ I'm a quadriplegic
- ☐ I'm physically disfigured
- ☐ I've lost a limb
- ☐ I have a debilitating disease
- ☐ I've been treated for emotional problems
- ☐ I've been persecuted for my beliefs
- ☐ I've had a serious illness
- ☐ I'm shy
- ☐ I'm adopted
- ☐ I'm an orphan
- ☐ I come from a single-parent home
- ☐ I've been abused
- ☐ I've been in trouble with the law
- ☐ I'm chemically dependent
- ☐ I'm homeless
- ☐ I have to take care of a parent or sibling
- ☐ I have a baby
- ☐ My family won't let me
- ☐ My family expects too much of me
- ☐ No one believes in me
- ☐ People have convinced me I can't
- ☐ I can't do it because…
- ☐ Other _____

How valid are your excuses? Turn the page.

They Did It in Spite of . . .

. . . PHYSICAL CHALLENGES

Jim Abbott, born with only one hand, won 12 baseball games in his rookie season as a pitcher with the California Angels.

Elliott Yamin, who is 90% deaf in his right ear, was one of three top finalists on the 2006 season of *American Idol*. His first album debuted at number three on *The Billboard 200* chart.

Stephen Hawking, Lucasian Professor of Mathematics at Cambridge University and considered the most brilliant theoretical physicist since Einstein, has ALS or Lou Gehrig's disease. He cannot walk or speak, but communicates through a computer attached to his wheelchair.

Winston Churchill, one of the greatest orators of the twentieth century, had a serious speech impediment.

President **Franklin Roosevelt** had polio and was unable to walk.

Ludwig von Beethoven was totally deaf when he composed some of his greatest music.

John Milton, one of the most renowned poets of all time, was blind.

Actor **Michael J. Fox** was diagnosed with young-onset Parkinson's disease in 1991, but continued to act until he retired from the award-winning *Spin City* in 2000. Still in demand as an actor, he now devotes much of his time to a foundation he started to raise funding for Parkinson's research.

Philippe Croizon swam across the English Channel, despite having lost both of his arms and both of his legs after a severe electric shock.

Mario Lemieux, Hockey Hall of Famer, Olympic Gold Medalist, and winner of two Stanley Cups, was diagnosed in 1993 with Hodgkin's disease. The same day he underwent his final radiation treatment, he played in a game against the Philadelphia Flyers, scoring a goal and an assist.

Stevie Wonder and the late **Ray Charles** are two of many blind musicians.

David Stevens, a thalidomide baby born without legs, became a high school wrestling champion, a college football player, and a skilled baseball player as well.

Known as the "Blade Runner," **Oscar Pistorius** was born without fibulae in both legs. When he was 11 months old, his legs were amputated halfway between his knees and ankles. Now a record-holding Paralympic runner, he is often referred to as "the fastest man with no legs."

. . . DISCRIMINATION OR OPPRESSION

Nelson Mandela remained the recognized leader of South African blacks despite spending more than 27 years as a political prisoner; he was elected President after his release.

Dith Pran escaped from a Khmer Rouge death camp in Cambodia and made his way to the United States, where he became a photographer for *The New York Times*.

Indira Gandhi of India and **Benazir Bhutto** of Pakistan became heads of state in two of the most male-dominated countries in the world. Gandhi was in her fourth term as Prime Minister when she was assassinated in 1984. After years in exile, Bhutto returned to Pakistan to work for free and fair elections. She was assassinated in December 2007.

Females receive 57% of all Bachelor's degrees, but only 18% of the engineering degrees.

... PERSONAL OR FAMILY PROBLEMS

Eleanor Roosevelt, painfully shy, orphaned, and considered unattractive, became not only First Lady of the United States, but a writer, speaker, political leader, and one of the most admired women in the world.

Albert Einstein was considered mentally dull as a youth.

Abraham Lincoln suffered bouts of severe depression throughout his life.

Olympic Gold Medalist **Greg Louganis's** dyslexia went unrecognized when he was a child. Because he stammered and was slower to learn, his classmates called him retarded. He was also adopted.

Joseph Fernandez, former Chanceller of the New York City public school system, was a member of a street gang and a high school dropout.

A recently divorced, single mom, **J.K. Rowling** was doing part-time clerical work and receiving welfare to make ends meet while completing her first *Harry Potter* novel. Her manuscript was rejected by 12 publishers before it finally got the green light. She is now the world's wealthiest novelist.

Mary Groda-Lewis was an elementary school dropout, street fighter, and juvenile offender. She had a stroke while giving birth and almost died, but she eventually received a high school equivalency degree and went to college. Determined to be a doctor, she was rejected by 15 medical schools before being accepted by Albany Medical College. She graduated from medical school at age 35.

Romano Banuelos, the thirty-seventh Treasurer of the United States, came to this country at age 16, when she was abandoned by her husband. She had seven dollars, two children, and no training. She did not speak English. Her first job was washing dishes, but with hard work and determination, she went on to become the manager of the largest Mexican wholesale food business in the world.

Lance Armstrong, after surviving a deadly cancer and aggressive chemotherapy, returned to competitive cycling and became the first person to win the grueling 21-day Tour de France *seven* consecutive years.

You can't change the circumstances of your birth, your family, or your past experiences. But, like many of the people on this chart, you can choose the way you let these things affect your life. You can concentrate on the things you cannot do. Many limitations are, after all, very real. Or you can make the most of the choices remaining to you. All of your opportunities lie in those areas that you can change, those places where you can act. Why waste energy on the rest? An old saying puts it well: "Give me the strength to change those things I can, the serenity to accept what can't be changed, and the wisdom to know the difference."

Do you know of any people in your own community who have overcome handicaps or adversities in their lives? If so, add their names below. These people are all heroes, and they can be inspiring role models.

_____

_____

It takes courage to be who you really are. It also takes a lot of effort.

Taking Responsibility

As you learned in chapter 8, *you* are responsible for directing your own life and solving your own problems. Trying to give that responsibility away (which is what you do when you make excuses) can get in the way of having the life you want. After all, if something isn't *your* problem, how can you solve it? But since it isn't *anyone else's* problem either, it doesn't get solved. It becomes a roadblock to your success.

The way to remove the roadblock is to take responsibility for it. Once you do that, you can usually think of ways to get around it or move it out of the way. For example, if you can't speak French because it's *too hard,* there's not much hope of ever learning French. But, when you say instead that you can't learn French because *you haven't put in the effort*, a remedy comes readily to hand. If you can't go to college because your parents can't afford to send you, there's not much hope of going to college. But if you can't go to college because you're not willing to work your way through or seek out financial aid, a number of solutions seem possible.

Can you think of any excuses you've made recently that made it seem something or someone else was responsible for your predicament? Write them below.

1. _____

2. _____

3. _____

Now analyze your own role in those situations and rewrite the statements, this time taking responsibility for the problem.

1. _____

2. _____

3. _____

STARTLING STATEMENT QUIZ

Circle the answer you think most accurately completes each of the following statements.

1. Each year _____ women under 20 in the United States become pregnant.
   a. 250,000
   b. 500,000
   c. 750,000
   d. 1 million

2. _____ percent of teen mothers graduate or earn a GED by the time they are 22 years old.
   a. 34
   b. 51
   c. 66
   d. 85

3. In 2009, _____ percent of families headed by a female lived in poverty.
   a. 12.7
   b. 21.6
   c. 29.9
   d. 40.9

4. In March 2011, the overall unemployment rate was 8.9 percent. For high school dropouts, the rate was _____ percent.
   a. 5.7
   b. 11.3
   c. 16.2
   d. 20.5

5. In 2009, _____ percent of blacks that did not complete high school lived in poverty. For those who completed college, the poverty rate was only
   a. 9.7
   b. 14.8
   c. 19.6
   d. 26.7

6. In 2009, _____ percent of 18- to 24-year-olds had left high school without a diploma.
   a. 2
   b. 9
   c. 13
   d. 20

7. In 2009, the median income for full-time workers 25 years and over with a bachelor's degree or more was $51,878 for women and $71,466 for men. The median income for workers with no high school diploma was _____ for women and _____ for men.
   a. $14,387 and $20,526
   b. $21,226 and $28,023
   c. $24,903 and $31,632
   d. $33,546 and $38,748

8. Teens that start drinking before the age of 14 are nearly _____ times more likely than adults that start drinking after they turn 21 to eventually become alcoholics.
   a. 3
   b. 4
   c. 6
   d. 7

9. _____ percent of the 33,808 total traffic fatalities in 2009 were caused by alcohol-related crashes.
   a. 14
   b. 23
   c. 32
   d. 41

10. The leading cause of death for 15- to 20-year-olds is motor vehicle crashes. In 2009, _____ percent of 15- to 20-year-old drivers who were killed in crashes were intoxicated.
   a. 7
   b. 15
   c. 24
   d. 32

11. While the use of many illicit drugs has dropped, abuse of marijuana is rising. In 2009, _____ percent of high school seniors reported using marijuana within the past month.
   a. 4.7
   b. 10.9
   c. 16.1
   d. 20.6

ANSWERS

1. c. There are about 750,000 teen pregnancies each year in the United States.[1] For these young women, many life choices are significantly diminished.

2. b. Only 51 percent of teen mothers completed high school or a GED.[2] For teen women who postponed pregnancy, 89 percent completed high school or a GED.

3. c. Among female-headed households, 29.9 percent had earnings below the poverty line.[3] The poverty rate for all segments of the population at that time was 17.3 percent. In other words, female-headed households are more than one and a half times as likely to be poor.

4. c. The unemployment rate for high school dropouts was 16.2 percent, much greater than the overall rate of 8.9 percent.[4] It is interesting to note that the unemployment rate for college graduates was only 4.7 percent.

5. d. The poverty rate for blacks who did not complete high school was 26.7 percent.[5] This is substantially higher than the overall poverty rate of 20.3 for folks of all races without a high school diploma. One of the best ways to fight discrimination is to be well educated and trained for employment.

6. b. Nearly one-tenth (9 percent) of all 18- and 24-year-olds had left school without getting a high school diploma in 2009.[6] Programs are available in all communities to help teens and young adults complete their education.

7. b. The median income in 2009 for women who had not completed high school was $21,226, while for men with no high school diploma it was $28,023.[7] Women especially need advanced education in order to earn a salary that will support a family adequately. Incidentally, women and men with less than a 9th grade education earned a median $18,480 and $23,945, respectively. For high school graduates, the median income was $29,150 for women and $39,478 for men.

8. d. 16.5 percent of teens who start drinking before the age of 14 will eventually become alcoholics, compared with 2.5 percent of adult who wait until the legal age of 21.[8] Alcohol abuse and dependency can reduce the quality of life; science has proven that it increases the chances of motor vehicle crashes, family violence, birth defects, liver disease, and various forms of cancer.

9. c. In 2009, 32 percent of all traffic fatalities were caused by alcohol-related crashes.[9] That means that an estimated 10,839 people died—or an average of one person every 75 minutes—as a result of these crashes.

10. c. For 15- to 20-year-old drivers in 2009, 24 percent of those killed in crashes had been drinking.[10] When alcohol is a factor in automobile accidents, the severity of the crash increases exponentially.

11. d. In 2009, 20.6 percent of high school seniors reported using marijuana within the past 30 days.[11] A survey of 8th, 10th, and 12th graders showed an increase in marijuana use along with corresponding decreases in peer disapproval and the perceived risk of the drug. Drug and alcohol use often leads to a significant drop in grades and, ultimately, expulsion. Refer back to answers 4, 5, and 7 to see how this could affect your future income. See answers 8, 9, and 10 to see how it could affect your life.

ARTIST'S NOTE: See page 285.

Detours and Roadblocks

Your teen years are likely to be among the most difficult and demanding in your life. Your friends may push you to do things that aren't in your best interests. Your parents might pressure you to achieve at school or in extracurricular activities. Perhaps you have to hold down a job, as well. Dating can be worrisome, and so can not dating. On top of everything else, this is a time you are making some decisions that will affect your entire future.

Sometimes it all seems too much. Why not just quit school or have a baby or start taking drugs? Wouldn't that relieve some of the pressure and pain?

Not for long. None of these behaviors can solve your problems. They can only delay their resolution. Short-term relief can lead to long-term regret.

Dana and Miko became friends in the second grade, when Dana's family moved in next door to Miko's. They were average students, but neither of them liked school very much. They had more fun in Dana's father's workshop, where they spent most of their summers taking things apart and putting them back together again. When Miko turned sixteen, she decided to quit school. It was boring and a waste of time, she said. Dana was tempted to join her, but she decided to stick it out. After graduation, she enrolled at the local vocational school and, within two years, was working as an electrician.

Who acted impulsively? In what way? _____

_____

Try to imagine what the future holds for Dana and Miko. Describe their lives 15 years later in the space below.

Dana's life: _____

_____

_____

Miko's life: _____

_____

_____

Josie and Juan went steady all through high school. So did Judy and Joe. During her senior year, Judy got pregnant and dropped out of school. She and Joe were married right after his graduation. Joe could not go to college to realize his dream—becoming a physical therapist—because he needed to work at a gas station to support his young family.

Josie and Juan were married after they graduated from college. Josie became a Certified Public Accountant, and Juan took a job as a high school teacher and coach.

Which couple acted impulsively? In what way? _____

_____

_____

What could life be like for these two couples in 15 years? Visualize their futures and describe them below.

Josie and Juan's life: _____

_____

_____

_____

_____

Judy and Joe's life: _____

_____

_____

_____

_____

205

Sam and Janice started experimenting with drugs when they were in the tenth grade. By the next year, drugs had become the focus of their lives. Both dropped out of school. When Sam was hospitalized after an overdose, he decided to get help. He entered a community treatment program and began attending night school. With his high school degree, he was able to get into the two-year training program offered by a large hotel chain. Within five years, Sam was assistant manager of the hotel, proud of his profession, and, most of all, proud of himself.

Janice never went back to school. Sam saw her once, waiting tables at the local diner. She looked tired and when she explained she was divorced and supporting her three children on her income alone, Sam understood why.

Who acted impulsively? In what way? _____

_____

Describe what you think Sam and Janice's lives might be like 15 years from now.

Sam's life: _____

_____

_____

_____

_____

Janice's life: _____

_____

_____

_____

_____

Is It Worth Staying in School?

You decide. Go back to pages 150–151. What careers did you say you might like? List them below.

_____

Imagine that you quit school before graduation. Could you qualify for any of these jobs without a high school diploma?

Yes   **No**

If so, which ones? _____

If not, you need another plan. Review the Your Personal Profile chart on page 27, your preferred lifestyle on page 63, your budget requirements on page 93 or your hardship budget on page 96, and your career portrait and priorities on page 134.

Now go through the career search process on pages 150–151 once more. This time, though, make sure that a high school diploma isn't required for the jobs you are investigating.

List three careers that meet your personal requirements but do not require a high school diploma below.

_____

Compare these jobs with the ones you listed at the top of the page. How are they different? Which careers do you think would be more satisfying? Why?

_____

_____

_____

_____

Imagine your life 15 years from now. What do you think it would be like if you take a job from your second list, the one that doesn't require a high school education? Which would you find more satisfying—a career from the first or second list?

_____

_____

_____

The Economics of Bad Habits

Bad habits (smoking, drinking, drugs, etc.) will affect your physical and mental health and, thus, your ability to achieve. They are, therefore, another roadblock to success.

You have probably heard most of the common arguments for staying away from harmful substances. Most people usually hesitate to start a harmful habit because of the physical danger involved. But have you ever considered the economics of your habit? If you haven't taken up any of these habits, the following exercise might motivate you to stay away from them. If you already use a harmful substance, it might motivate you to put some energy into giving it up.

Complete the chart below, using the following information:

You are 18 years old when you begin smoking and you continue to smoke a pack a day for the rest of your life. If you live to be the national average age of 78 years old (your chances of reaching this age are lower because of your habit, by the way) and a pack of cigarettes continues to cost $4.80,* how much will your habit cost every year? Every 10 years? How much over your lifetime? Can you think of any other ways you might like to spend this money?

	One pack/day	Other use for money
Cost/year	$	
Cost/10 years	$	
Cost/60 years	$	

* NOTE: $4.80 was the average price of a pack of cigarettes in the United States in 2010. Various state and local taxes cause this figure to vary greatly across the country. If you use smoking as your bad habit for the activity on page 209, you'll want to use the cost in your own state.

You will spend about $1,752 a year. That comes to $17,520 over 10 years, or $105,120 over 60 years.

Let's take our experiment one step further: If, between the ages of 18 and 65, you annually put $1,752 in a retirement account earning 8 percent interest,* that account would be worth $793,481 when you retire.

If you deposited your smoking money monthly instead of annually *($146 per month = $1,752 divided by 12 months)*, your account earning 8 percent interest* would be worth $907,007 when you turn 65.

In other words, if you saved the money you might have spent smoking, you would be able to retire with a guaranteed annual interest income (at 8 percent) of

> $63,478 per year if you made annual deposits, or
>
> $72,561 per year if you deposited your money monthly.

Some habits are much more expensive than cigarettes. Before you get involved with them, use the same equation to determine how much they would cost you over a lifetime.

Habit _____

Cost/day _____   Cost/week _____

Other use for money

Cost/year	$	
Cost/10 years	$	
Cost/60 years	$	

* NOTE: Over the last two decades interest rates on investment accounts have fluctuated between 14% and 1%. We have chosen 8% as an average. You can find the current interest rates for a variety of available investment options on the Internet. You'll also find many useful online calculators for factoring retirement savings.

If You've Decided to Give Up Your Dream

Evie always wanted to be a journalist. She did very well in college. Her teachers encouraged her in her plans. Then, two quarters before graduation, Evie quit college and married her high school sweetheart. She told everyone she'd changed her mind about journalism, that this was what she really wanted. Deep in her heart, though, she wasn't sure why she decided to give up her dream.

Keith wanted to be a social worker, but his parents always assumed he would take over the family business. He tried to talk with them about his plans, but they just didn't understand. The business they had worked so hard to build could not last without his help, they said. Keith decided he owed it to his family to obey their wishes.

Carlotta changed her mind about becoming a research scientist when she took a look at the class requirements. How could she ever pass all those math tests? She might as well forget the whole idea, she told herself.

Sometimes there are good reasons to give up your dream. If your eyesight doesn't meet FAA standards, for example, you may as well forget about being a pilot. If the factory that has employed several generations of workers in your town closes its doors, you need an alternate plan. Or, if you come across an intriguing idea you hadn't thought of before, you owe it to yourself to give this new dream serious consideration.

Often, however, people give up too soon or for the wrong reasons. Usually, if they look more closely, these people find that they are acting out of fear.

Fear can take many forms. It can feel like obligation. It can feel like loss of interest. It can even feel like falling in love. Are you giving up on your dream because of fear? Consider the possibility carefully, especially if one or more of the following categories applies to you.

If You're A Woman

In a study of high school valedictorians, researchers at the University of Illinois found that, during their college careers, the young women in the group tended to scale back the ambitions they had on the day they graduated from high school. It wasn't because of their grades. In fact, the females were getting consistently better grades than the males in the group. So why were they changing their plans while the males remained more dedicated to their goals? There are several possible answers.

Some women still think it's not "feminine" to be ambitious or successful at work. They are afraid that success on the job will take a heavy toll on their personal life—that they will not have the time or energy to marry or have children. This fear, however, is largely unfounded. Today, 79 percent of women with children over the age of 6 work for pay, and men are more and more likely to expect their wives to help support the family.

Women who plan to balance their careers with marriage and children may also believe that scaling back their plans for work will make them better mothers. In fact, though, women who prepare for the more demanding careers usually earn more and have more flexibility in their work lives—and these things help them be the kind of mother they want to be.

Let's explore this concept further. Do you think the workers in each of the careers below are mostly men or mostly women? In the first column, beside each job title, write an F if you believe more females work in this field, an M if you think more men do.

Now go back and circle the careers that would probably offer the most flexible hours. In other words, which workers could most easily decide to take time off in the afternoon to attend a son or daughter's basketball game? Some careers are decidedly more flexible than others.

_____ Child care worker	_____ Architect
_____ Office clerks, general	_____ Auto body repairer
_____ Cashier	_____ Chemical engineer
_____ Janitor	_____ Computer programmer
_____ Nurse (RN)	_____ Air traffic controller
_____ Plumber	_____ Securities sales representative
_____ Elementary school teacher	_____ Chiropractor (self-employed)

Child care worker	$18,605	
Office clerks, general	$25,320	
Cashier	$17,320	
Janitor	$21,032	
Nurse (RN)	$62,450	
Plumber	$44,758	
Elementary school teacher	$47,100	

Architect	$70,320
Auto body repairer	$36,332
Chemical engineer	$74,600
Computer programmer	$69,620
Air traffic controller	$111,870
Securities sales representative	$68,680
Chiropractor (self-employed)	$94,454

Source: U.S. Department of Labor, Bureau of Labor Statistics, *Occupational Outlook Handbook,* 2010–2011 Edition.

Along the bottom of the following graph, first list the careers that are held mostly by women, beginning on the left-hand bottom column. We've already included the child care worker and office clerk as examples. Next add the jobs held mostly by men. Now, star the flexible careers, jobs in which workers can choose their own hours. We've used the chiropractor as an example.

$120,000 plus

$115,000
$110,000
$105,000
$100,000
$95,000
$90,000
$85,000
$80,000
$75,000
$70,000
$65,000
$60,000
$55,000
$50,000
$45,000
$40,000
$35,000
$30,000
$25,000
$20,000
$15,000
$10,000
$5,000

Child care worker

Office clerk

*Chiropractor

Now use a pencil to chart the annual average salaries of the flexible careers. Use a pen to chart the annual average salaries of the non-flexible careers. (Note: The salaries we've used come from Department of Labor sources. Individuals might be able to earn a higher salary by working freelance or starting their own small businesses.)

Suppose a woman with three children suddenly found herself the sole support of her family. Decide what a family this size in your community needs a year to live in minimal comfort.

$ _____ per year

Now, draw a double line across the chart at this dollar level.

Which careers from the list would be most suitable for parenting? That is, which would provide both flexibility and an adequate salary? List those careers below. (Hint: These careers are graphed in pencil, above the double line.)

_____

_____

Which of the careers on your list require either a college or vocational degree or some other type of special training? Circle them.

Do more men or women currently hold these jobs?

More men   More women

Role models are important, and in many careers women still have fewer of them than men. Consequently, it may be more difficult for young women to visualize themselves being successful as engineers, contractors, or computer specialists. As graduation draws near, panic may set in. It may suddenly seem more appealing to be a receptionist rather than an engineer, a teacher rather than a computer programmer. However, an impulsive change in direction could be costly for your future family.

REMEMBER: The higher you go on the career ladder, the more flexibility you will have for parenting. When you earn a higher wage, you may be able to afford to work less than full time. Highly trained professionals also usually have more freedom to set their own hours.

A note to young men: It's also to your benefit to encourage the young women in your life. When both partners in a household are capable of supporting the family financially, men have more freedom to enrich their own lives. For example, they might go back to school, or take time out to stay home with children. They have more freedom to change careers, or to work at a job they love that doesn't support the family at the desired level. Or, if they are unable to work for any reason, they can rest assured that the family will be okay.

IF YOU'RE "THE FIRST IN THE FAMILY" OR IF YOUR FAMILY DOES NOT SUPPORT YOUR DREAM

Some parents place a great deal of importance on education. Even if they did not graduate from high school or attend college themselves, they applaud the ambitions and abilities of their children. And that makes things easier for the younger generation. In other families, parents may be quietly proud of their children. Or they may not see the point of further education. They might even think of school as a waste of time. In these situations, it is more difficult for sons and daughters to pursue their dreams. To do so might feel like betraying the family. But it is not disloyal to yourself. Although you may run the risk of losing their support, the true betrayal is to give up on yourself and your aspirations.

A similar—and perhaps even more difficult—problem arises when parents disapprove of your chosen career, or have other plans for your future: you should be a doctor, not an artist; you should take over the family business instead of starting a flower shop. Your parents, of course, have reasons for thinking as they do. And you should listen to them respectfully. But, in the end, it is your life—and you are ultimately responsible for your life's satisfaction or dissatisfaction.

Without a doubt, it is easier to achieve your goals when you have the support of people you love and respect. If you cannot get that support at home, try to get it elsewhere. See pages 262–263 about locating mentors.

IF YOU DON'T THINK YOU DESERVE IT

No one can make you feel inferior without your consent.

— Eleanor Roosevelt

Remember the message center exercise on pages 50-53? What kinds of messages have you been getting about your future prospects? If any of them are negative ("You'll never amount to anything") or limiting ("remember your place"), you may have to fight periods of self-doubt and low self-esteem. At these times, it may seem like a good idea to give up and prove that the messengers are right: you are a failure and you don't deserve to succeed. A better idea is to acknowledge the messages, thank them for their input, and get on about your business.

Some people send *themselves* messages about their own worthiness. With so many poor, homeless, and starving people in the world, they reason, they have no right to pursue an economically rewarding career. Of course, it is important to be concerned about other people's needs. But, in fact, you can't solve many problems by becoming a victim yourself. Remember that, when you do achieve your goal, you will be in a better position to help others or to work for social change.

BEFORE YOU GIVE UP

Can you think of a dream or ambition you had in the past that you have abandoned? Something you wanted to do or accomplish? Perhaps you dreamed of singing a solo in the school concert or asking your neighbor to the Spring dance. Maybe, while watching *Law & Order* you've dreamed of becoming an attorney.

Think of a dream that you have given up or are considering giving up? (If you haven't given your dreams much thought, now is the time to start thinking about them seriously. Try to write them down when they come to mind.)

Before you decide to give up something you once thought you wanted badly, answer the following questions.

What was your old dream? _____

How long did you hold it? _____

When did you decide to give up your dream? _____

Why? _____

What is your new dream? _____

Why does it appeal to you now? _____

Is there hard evidence to support your decision to give up your dream (you can't carry a tune, you've flunked out of school, you've run out of money, etc.)?

_____

If so, is this just an obstacle, or have you really reached the end of the road?

_____

If there is no hard evidence, have you discussed your decision with your teachers or your advisor? What do they think?

_____

If you've come up against an obstacle, would you hang on to your dream if the obstacle would simply disappear (the math requirement is lifted, you win the sweepstakes)?

_____

If you've decided to give up your dream because of some rational obstacle (money, grades), think of as many possible ways to overcome your problem as you can. List them below. Are any of them workable?

_____

_____

If your reasons for giving up your dream are weak, your decision may be based on fear or anxiety. In the story on page 210, for example, Carlotta decided not to become a research scientist because she is anxious about math. She didn't fail at math. Her fear kept her from even trying to get through it.

Try not to let this happen to you. The truth is, everyone has anxieties. Trying to avoid situations that might make you feel uncomfortable can put unnecessary constraints on your life. The best thing to do is to learn how to tolerate the feelings that come with being ill at ease. If you can experience the anxiety (go to the party, get on the airplane), you will gradually overcome it.

By avoiding the thing that made her anxious, Carlotta deprived herself of that opportunity. What if she had signed up for a math class instead? Is there anything she could have done to lessen her anxiety?

She might have tried visualization. This is a technique that allows you to think about the thing you fear in great detail over a period of time. As you do this, you become less sensitive to the object of your fear and more confident about your abilities to deal with the situation.

CONQUERING YOUR FEARS

If you, like Carlotta, suffer from math anxiety, try this exercise. Start by relaxing. It's important to feel at ease. Visualize yourself entering the classroom and taking a seat. See yourself listening to the lecture and understanding what is being said. Allow yourself to experience your feelings when the first test is announced. Then think about a time when you were up against something you were sure you couldn't do but, with hard work and concentration, did successfully. Now see yourself studying for the test. Visualize taking your seat on exam day, picking up your pencil, reading the questions, and completing every problem.

If you repeat this exercise daily for several weeks, you should begin to feel more comfortable with the subject. When that happens, you will become more confident, and that should help you perform better in the real class, as well. (You can't just see yourself studying, however. You have to actually do it!)

Write a guided visualization below that might help you conquer a fear you currently have. Try to see yourself actually doing whatever it is that makes you anxious and write the process below.

One Step At A Time

SALLY'S STORY

At first, Sally was delighted to be offered a full scholarship to a top-rated college. But then the anxiety set in: The college was way across the country, and she had never been away from home before. She'd never even been on an airplane (that was another fear). And what if the other students didn't like her? After all, her family had no money or social standing, while many of her classmates would be wealthy socialites. She was tempted to turn down the scholarship. But she knew the education she could get there would help prepare her for law school and her dream—becoming a civil rights lawyer and, perhaps, eventually, a Supreme Court justice.

Sally's school counselor, Mr. Chan, had a suggestion: "Why don't you make a list of five or six things that frighten you?" he said. Sally thought about the assignment overnight, then wrote down her concerns:

Fear of flying

Fear of living so far from home

Fear of being an outsider because of my background

Fear of public speaking

Fear of confronting a friend who betrayed a confidence

Fear of failing my driver's test

"Okay," said Mr. Chan when she returned the next day. "Now rearrange your list. Put the item that concerns you least at the top and work your way down toward the situation that causes you the most anxiety."

That was easy enough, Sally decided:

1. Fear of confronting my friend

2. Fear of failing my driver's test

3. Fear of feeling like an outsider

4. Fear of public speaking

5. Fear of flying

6. Fear of living away from home

"Now what am I supposed to do?" she asked.

"Many people find they can overcome their fears by taking them on one at a time, from easiest to most difficult," said Mr. Chan. "So your job is to take care of the first item on your list as soon as possible. Then do the second, and so on.

"It's sort of like a baby learning to walk. First you learn to creep, next you crawl, and then you stand up. Finally, you're ready to take the big step. But the earlier trials help you gain the skills and confidence you need to succeed."

That night, Sally couldn't get to sleep. How could she confront her friend? It made her head ache and her stomach queasy. She didn't like the feeling at all, but she did talk to Lynn the next morning. Afterwards, Sally was relieved—and very pleased with herself. She had done it! She'd faced her fear and kept her friendship intact as well!

Feeling more confident now, she made an appointment to take her driver's test two weeks later. She reviewed the manual, visualized passing the test, and got her mother to promise she'd practice driving with Sally for at least five hours before the exam. When Sally passed, she started to feel as though she could continue mastering her anxieties and gained a new sense of personal strength.

Next on her list, Sally had to learn that she could feel at ease with, and be accepted by, people from different backgrounds. She was invited to the mayor's reception for outstanding students, though she hadn't planned to go. Now, however, it seemed like a good opportunity. Sally decided to put aside her usual shyness and talk with everyone in the room. She felt self-conscious at first, but before long she was more comfortable and found herself behaving more confidently.

The next step, however, seemed more of a problem. For Sally, speaking with people one-on-one was quite different from addressing a crowd. Since this was a more difficult situation, she made another visit to Mr. Chan.

"Sometimes we have to break things down even further," he said. "These challenges can't be bridged all at once. It takes time to overcome them. I suggest you come up with a step-by-step plan that will lead you to speaking in public, say, within two months.

"Try visualizing yourself in the situation, thinking through the various steps. Practice this three times a day while you're relaxed until you are comfortable with the feeling."

Sally decided her first step would be to volunteer an answer in math class every day for a week. She practiced visualizing raising her hand and speaking until she felt ready to try it. It was uncomfortable the first day, but within a week it seemed more natural.

That gave her the courage to register for a speech class beginning the following month. Until it started, Sally kept volunteering answers in her other classes. At least once a day, she also visualized doing well in the speech class.

After the first day of speech class, when everyone had left the room, Sally went up on stage and stood behind the lectern. She pretended to adjust the microphone, and looked out over the auditorium. Her imaginary audience applauded her wildly.

Finally, the day came. Sally was well prepared for her speech. The class didn't respond as she had hoped but, when she thought things through, Sally decided she had done what she wanted to do. She could feel good about herself. And, the next time she got up to speak, the class did respond to her noticeable improvement.

By this time, Sally was beginning to get a sense of herself as one who could achieve her other needs as long as she was willing to face and work through her discomfort. She began looking forward to her flight as one more in a series of heroic adventures...a challenge that she could conquer. She also began to feel she would be able to deal with the problems she would encounter in her new life at college. There would be times when she'd be homesick, she knew. And she would certainly be frightened or nervous about the many new situations coming her way. But she also was learning she could tolerate discomfort and, if she faced it squarely, it would eventually diminish so she could get on with her goal: Getting the best education she could, and realizing her dream.

YOUR COURAGE ACTION PLAN

Like Sally, you may be facing a number of situations that make you uncomfortable or afraid. Some of them may even tempt you to give up your dream. List five fears you have or situations you are avoiding.

1. _____

2. _____

3. _____

4. _____

5. _____

Which of these do you think would be easiest for you to overcome? Which would be hardest? List your fears again, starting with the situation that causes you the least anxiety and working toward the item that makes you feel most uncomfortable.

1. _____

2. _____

3. _____

4. _____

5. _____

Think of a plan you could use to confront the first two items on your list. Write your plan below.

_____

_____

_____

_____

Once you put your plans into action, record your feelings and experiences in the space provided.

_____

_____

_____

YORIK'S STORY

Yorik was born in Yerp, a tiny country on the Yorta Sea. Yerp is a beautiful place, and the Yerpese are generally a very happy people. Their main industry is raising yaks—wooly, horned cattle—for the production of yak yarn and yak yogurt.

Yorik, unfortunately, is allergic to yaks and everything yakish. As such, his future in Yerp is limited. He is an ambitious young man, however, and decides that, if he is ever going to realize his dreams (and maybe even stop sneezing)—he would have to leave Yerp. So, one day, he kisses his parents good-bye and gets on a boat to America.

Yorik arrives in the United States alone and with little money. He doesn't know anyone here. He has little education, and just a limited knowledge of English. But he is healthy (at last!) and ambitious, determined to make a good life for himself. He thinks he should be able to accomplish his goals within ten years.

What advice would you give Yorik? His career and lifestyle goal is listed below with a sample of his first year objectives. As Yorik's career counselor, write a 10-year plan that you think would help him achieve his goals. Include objectives for education or training, living arrangements, employment, and finances. (Do you remember the components of an objective? The diagrams we've used as an example should refresh your memory.)

Yorik's goal: At the end of ten years, to speak English fluently, hold a satisfying job that I have trained for, own a home, and have $5,000 in savings.

Year one:

Education or training: To take English classes twice a week all year long.

Living arrangements: To rent a small, inexpensive apartment and, within two weeks, find two roommates.

Employment: Within 30 days, to find a fulltime job I qualify for that pays at least $10 an hour.

Finances: To save $3,000 for education or training within two years.

Write your 10-year plan for Yorik:

Year one:

Education and training: _____

Living arrangements: _____

Employment: _____

Finances: _____

Year three:

Education and training: _____

Living arrangements: _____

Employment: _____

Finances: _____

Year five:

Education and training: _____

Living arrangements: _____

Employment: _____

Finances: _____

Year eight:

Education and training: _____

Living arrangements: _____

Employment: _____

Finances: _____

Year ten:

Education and training: _____

Living arrangements: _____

Employment: _____

Finances: _____

How did Yorik delay gratification in the plan you just described? _____

_____

How might he have acted impulsively? _____

_____

Did he take responsibility for himself?   Yes   No

What excuses might a less determined person have made? _____

_____

What anxieties might he have had to overcome? _____

223

Taking Risks

Research shows that there are, basically, two different kinds of people when it comes to taking risks. Some people have a high need for achievement and are able to set and meet progressively more difficult goals. They see risk taking as a challenge and a learning experience. Others, afraid of failing, either take very small risks that teach them nothing or set their goals so high that no one could expect them to succeed. Their anxiety prevents them from growing and learning. Fortunately, since calculated risk taking is an important skill for successful living, it is possible to improve your ability to perform this task.

As a skill, risk taking combines the techniques for overcoming anxieties and making decisions. By definition, a risk involves uncertainty or danger. There is the possibility of losing something or suffering some kind of harm. It is reasonable, therefore, to be apprehensive. But taking a risk is also like making a decision. You choose to do it only when you have determined your goal, examined the alternatives, evaluated the pros and cons, and considered the probability of success. If, after going through that process, you decide the possible outcome is worth the risk, you need to trust in your ability to handle your fears and the discomfort they create—and go for it.

The inability to take calculated risks can be just as paralyzing as the inability to overcome fears. When you use the decision-making model, however, you will often find that the risk is a relatively small one. What is the worst thing that could happen if you ask someone for a date, for example? (Hint: It should not be the end of life on this planet. Nor should it brand you forever as a hopeless geek with a talent for self-deception. Try to evaluate which part of your anxiety is real, and which part is not.) The worst that could happen is that the other person will decline your offer, and then you will get on with your life.

Are you willing to take that chance? Perhaps not. It might be more important for you to hang on to the dream that he or she is harboring a secret passion for you than to actually have a date with this person. This is another point to keep in mind. Know what you are willing to risk or lose. Analyze the probability of the worst happening. And, if there seems to be a good possibility of losing something you hold dear, don't take the chance.

Here are some other points to consider about taking risks.

1. Don't try to solve *emotional* problems with *physical* risks. You can't solve the problems you have with your parents, for example, by driving carelessly, drinking or taking drugs, or risking pregnancy.

2. Make sure you take your **own** risks, not someone else's. And don't let anyone else take your risks for you. You will not be totally committed to a goal that is not your own. And you can't expect someone else to feel as strongly about your goals as you do. In either case, the risk is likely to fail. (Example: A business is failing. Two people could possibly save it. Assuming they have comparable abilities, who do you think would be more successful, the person who owns the business, or the one who has no financial or emotional investment in it?)

3. Taking risks *does not* mean taking unnecessary chances. Young people, especially, are prone to taking hazardous risks in order to *prove themselves*. In truth, however, they prove little except their own lack of understanding. The only kind of risk worth taking is one that takes you a step closer to your stated goal.

4. Taking a risk is taking action. You cannot get to the place you want to be by simply wishing.

5. Do not take a risk unless you are willing to *make your best effort*. Commit yourself to your goal. As David Viscott says in his book, *Risking,* "If you don't intend to succeed, you intend to fail."

Getting Back on Track
If You've Derailed

The advice on the preceding pages may be helpful if you are only thinking of giving up your dream, or if you've been temporarily sidetracked. However, sometimes people get derailed, and they need more help than we can provide in these pages.

That doesn't mean their lives are hopeless, not by any means. Reconsider the stories on pages 204–206, for example. Maybe Miko went back to night school to earn her high school diploma. Perhaps Judy did the same, and then she and Joe shared childcare duties and worked part-time while going on to college or vocational school. Janice might have become an apprentice and learned a skilled craft that paid well enough for her to support her family more comfortably. All of them, though, would need guidance and assistance.

If you've quit school, if you're taking drugs, if you're pregnant or raising a child, or if you simply feel lost or abandoned, you may think your future is hopeless. **It's not**, but you must seek out the help you need to get back on track.

Can your parents help? They are probably just as worried as you are about your situation. If you don't feel you can go to them, there are other resources. People who know and care about you are often in the best position to give support, so consider talking with a favorite teacher or coach, a school counselor, your minister, priest, or rabbi, or another adult you trust and respect. If you prefer to remain anonymous, consider calling local agencies such as the United Way, Alcoholics Anonymous, the Y's, Family Services, and Community Counseling Centers. Whatever you do, don't do it alone. Get help! And one way you can help yourself is to remember this: When sitting on the bottom rung of the career ladder, the only available direction is up.

Amira dreamed of becoming a doctor since she was a little girl. However, along the way she lost track of that dream and dropped out of high school. Deep down she was still fascinated with medicine, so she went to the local hospital to look for work. Although the only job she qualified for was as a cashier in the gift shop, she remembered her vision and made a commitment to put the energy into getting the education she needed to realize her dream.

Most people would think that Amira's future looks pretty bleak, but she doesn't have to buy into their assessment. She can still reach her dream if she is willing to set a goal, develop a plan, and work at getting the education and training necessary to achieve it. Even if she doesn't become a doctor, the following career ladder will help her visualize her alternatives based on her commitment to education and training.

CAREER BACK-UP PLAN

Keeping your own career area of interest in mind, map out career alternatives based on the chart below. We've included Amira's chart to use as a guide along with an example for someone interested in teaching*.

1. First, write your ideal job title in the box that corresponds with the required training or education. Use a different color pen or all capital letters for that one box.

2. In the *starred* box ★, write the industry or career cluster with which this career is affiliated.

3. Based on the different commitments to education and training (column 1), choose at least one other job within that career interest area and put that job title in the corresponding box, along with the annual median salary. The *Occupational Outlook Handbook,* print or online (see page 148), will be your best resource.

ALTERNATIVE CAREER LADDER						
Education/Training Level	Job Title	Median Annual Salary	Job Title	Median Annual Salary	Job Title	Median Annual Salary
	HEALTH SERVICES		EDUCATION		★	
Doctoral or Professional Degree	**DOCTOR**	$186,044	**District Superintendent**	$159,634		
Masters Degree	**Nurse Practitioner**	$ 82,590	**School Principal**	$ 83,880		
Bachelor + Work Experience or Certification	**Medical Sonographer**	$ 61,980	**Special Ed Teacher**	$ 50,020		
Bachelor Degree	**Registered Nurse**	$ 62,450	**SCHOOL TEACHER**	$ 53,150		
Associate Degree	**Medical Assistant**	$ 28,300	**Payroll Clerk**	$ 34,810		
Postsecondary Vocational Certificate	**Medical Transcriber**	$ 32,053	**Executive Secretary**	$ 40,030		
Long-term on-the-job training	**Pharmacy Technician**	$ 27,706	**Cafeteria Cook**	$ 20,460		
Moderate-term on-the-job training	**Pharmacy Aide**	$ 20,093	**Child Care Worker**	$ 21,902		
Short-term on-the-job training	**Home Care Aide**	$ 19,178	**School Bus Driver**	$ 26,603		
No High School Diploma	**Gift Shop Cashier**	$ 17,659	**School Janitor**	$ 22,145		

— Do you see alternative careers that you might consider? Which ones and why?

— What if you were going to school, ran out of money, and needed to go to work for a period of time? Would one of the job titles listed below your ideal career make sense for the short-term? Why or why not?

— What other observations can you surmise from this data? Study your chart and discuss your conclusions with friends and mentors.

* NOTE: The education and training required, as well as the median annual salary levels, will vary from state to state. These are national averages.

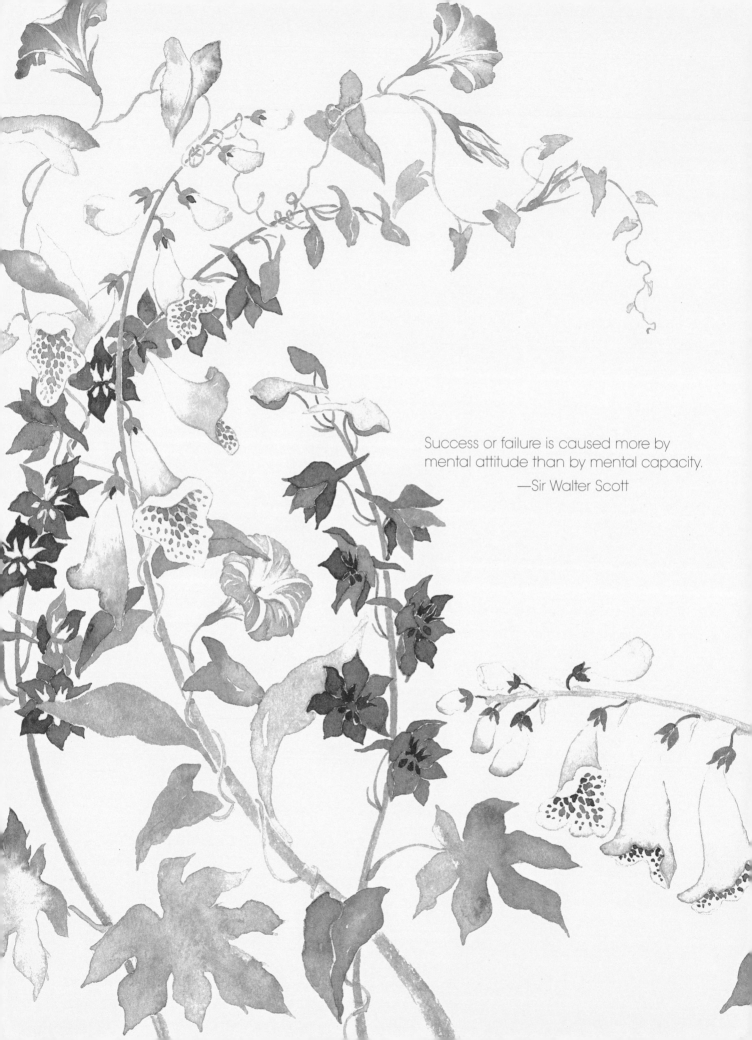

Success or failure is caused more by
mental attitude than by mental capacity.
—Sir Walter Scott

CHAPTER TEN

Attitude Is Everything

Learning to accentuate the positive

Think you can or think you can't, either
way you will be right.
— Henry Ford

Section Three:
HOW DO I GET IT?

The attitude of success:
Self-confidence: "I can do it!"
Perseverance: "It can be done!"
Desire: "I'm going to do it!"

According to the old nutritionists' saying, "you are what you eat." Most people feel more like a hero or a failure or a nice guy than they do like a peanut butter sandwich, so more accurate saying might be, "you are what you think you are."

Attitude is everything. Muhammad Ali was telling the world "I am the greatest" long *before* he became heavyweight boxing champion. In the movie *Funny Girl,* the Fanny Brice character played by Barbra Streisand sings "I'm the Greatest Star" *before* she becomes just that. During the worst days of the Great Depression, one of the most popular songs was "Happy Days are Here Again," and soon they were.

It may seem unlikely, but it works: Telling yourself that you are the kind of person you want to become—acting as though you are that person *now*—helps you achieve your goals. Pretending is a way of practicing. And, without practice, how would we learn to do all the wonderful things we do?

The late actor Cary Grant once said, "I pretended to be somebody I wanted to be, and I finally became that person." In other words, pretending something is true can make it so. Perhaps this is not so surprising. If you want to become more confident, for example, *pretending* that you already are will probably lead to some kind of reward: getting the job or the date or the good grade on your speech. That experience will help *make* you more confident, which will help you keep up your act. As you continue to pile up rewards, you will do increasingly less acting. Soon, you may just find that you have *become a confident person.*

Affirmations Promote Action

Your life is an expression of all your thoughts.
— Marcus Aurelius

Another way to change your attitude is by using affirmations. Think back to the Positive Messages to Yourself exercise on page 53. Affirmations are like the messages you get from other important people in your life, but they come from you—the most important person of all. You can tell yourself anything you like. Since the other messages reached you first, however, it will take time and constant repetition to replace them with new ones.

In order to be most effective, affirmations should also:

1. Be said aloud and repeated throughout the day, or written down. It's even more effective to record them and listen to them while you're in a semi-hypnotic state such as running or lying down.

2. Include your name. "I, _____, am a good student."

3. Be in the present tense. Say that the condition you hope to bring about is true **now!**

4. Be short, positive, and clear. "I, Waldo, am a graceful dancer" is better than "I, Waldo, am going to stop stepping on people's feet, tripping on my shoelaces, and running into the concession stand."

5. Be meaningful and believable to you!

What affirmations can you write about your future? In making your decision, consider reversing any negative messages from the exercise on page 52. For example, if your message from your father is "You can't do anything right," you might include an affirmation that states "I, Violeta, can do anything I set my mind to." If you've received the message "You'll never be good at math," you could benefit from an affirmation stating "I, LeeAnn, am a good math student."

We've included a few statements as examples. Use them if they could be helpful for you. Then write your own affirmations in the space below. Repeat them to yourself often. Act as if they are true now.

I, _____, am confident when meeting new people.

I, _____, am capable of getting a good job.

I, _____, am good at making and keeping friends.

I, _____, am _____

I, _____, am _____

I, _____, am _____

The Six Es of Excellence

If a man has good corn, or wood, or boards, or pigs to sell, or can make better chairs or knives, crucibles, or church organs, than anybody else, you will find a broad, hard-beaten road to his house, though it be in the woods.
— Ralph Waldo Emerson

Nothing great will ever be achieved without great people, and people are great only if they are determined to be so.
— Charles de Gaulle

Good is not good where better is expected.
— Thomas Fuller

To excel means to do something of superior quality, to be the best that you can be—to know you've given your all to the task. By setting high standards and putting in an unusual amount of effort, an individual can go a long way toward assuring a quality existence.

Remember the formula for success from chapter 1:

$$\text{VISION} + \text{ENERGY} = \text{SUCCESS}$$

The formula for excellence takes this one step further:

HIGH STANDARDS + UNUSUAL EFFORTS = EXCELLENCE

This principle holds true in any line of work. By being the best cook or plumber or accountant in town, you can expect to live well. Better still, you can expect to be respected and to have a sense of personal satisfaction.

We want quality in the products and services we buy—even if we have to pay more for them. Doesn't it follow, then, that we should be just as concerned about excellence in the work we do and the way we live our lives? Satisfaction comes, ultimately, not simply from doing something, but from doing something well.

But excellence requires a conscious and ongoing commitment, a willingness to set high standards and exert unusual efforts. Not everyone is willing to sustain this kind of commitment. How do you acquire excellence? For starters, you can apply the following principles to your life, whether it's the work you do or the plans you make—alone and as part of a team.

As you evaluate your own efforts or that of any team, use the following qualities as your guide. Incorporate these standards into your work and there is a greater chance you'll meet your goals in an admirable fashion.

> Note: It's important to keep in mind that a team's success depends on all members sharing a common understanding of the importance of these characteristics.

EXPECTATIONS

The dictionary says that the word expectation "suggests anticipation of success or fulfillment." Actually, it's another word for vision. Expectations are often self-fulfilling prophecies—if you expect to be happy and successful, you have a good chance of achieving your goals. But, if you expect a poor outcome, that's about what you're likely to get.

Therefore, it is important to have high expectations—for yourself and from yourself. Many people shortchange themselves by expecting only what they think is possible in a negative sense, or what others think they *should* want. Quite often, good students to whom learning comes easily believe that everything should be easy. When they come up against a task that requires effort on their part, such as learning to play a sport, they give up. They aren't used to making an effort to succeed, so they limit their expectations to those things that they can do most easily.

What should you expect? Review your answers to the exercises in chapter 3. Expect to get what you said you want.

ENTHUSIASM

Once your expectations are in place, it's easier to generate the enthusiasm you need to accomplish your goals. Enthusiasm is the eagerness, interest, or excitement with which you approach a job or activity. It grows out of knowing what you want and doing what you love. If you have always dreamed of being a teacher, for example, your enthusiasm is likely to show up in your lectures and lesson plans. And you will probably be good at and happy in your job. If you really wanted to be a fire fighter, however, but went into teaching because that's what your parents wanted you to do, you aren't likely to have the same enthusiasm. You won't enjoy your job as much, and you won't do it as well as some others will.

This is the basic thesis of Marsha Sinetar's book *Do What You Love, The Money Will Follow*. When you "discover your right livelihood," as she puts it, your enthusiasm will help assure that you give the job the time and attention it requires if you are to excel at it.

Of course, people don't always land their ideal job—at least, not right away. But if you can work up some enthusiasm for the work you do, you have a much better chance of moving beyond it to something more challenging and rewarding.

Author Brenda Ueland once said, "Never do anything you don't want to do." Few of us can follow that advice in all aspects of our lives, but it is something to keep in mind. Enthusiasm is the breath of life that can make even the most mundane tasks rewarding. When you plan your career, aim to do something you love, something you value. If you do that, your chances of excelling will increase because of your enthusiasm (love) for your project.

Nothing great was ever achieved without enthusiasm.
— Ralph Waldo Emerson

ENERGY

You can spend the rest of your life daydreaming about your future—or you can make your dreams happen. But it takes energy to put your plans into action. Fortunately, if you are enthused about what you are doing, the energy will usually come.

Everyone, though, has days when it's hard to get going. Of course, it's a good idea to take a day off now and again. But how do you overcome inertia when you know you need to get something done?

First, try repeating your version of the statements on page 121: "I want _____ , therefore, I should _____." If that doesn't work, try easing yourself into the chore. Promise yourself that if you do one small part of the project, or work on it for a short period of time (half an hour?), you can quit. Often, once you get going, the energy will start flowing and you will be able to accomplish much more than you hoped. Finally, if all else fails, "just do it," as they say.

Of course, everyone has only so much energy. It's important to set your priorities and do the most important projects first. Otherwise, they may not get done at all. There are many ways to waste time enjoyably. You should make time to do just that. But, generally, your life will be more productive and your free time more enjoyable if you do the things you must do first. That way, you can spend the remaining time any way you like, without worry.

Keep in mind, too, that energy springs from good health. Without adequate rest, nutrition, and exercise, it is difficult to maintain your energy level.

ENTERPRISE

By "enterprise" we mean the willingness to take calculated risks, the ability to recognize both problems and opportunities, and the creativity to make the best of either situation. The old saying, "When life gives you a lemon, make lemonade," was undoubtedly coined by an enterprising person.

This quality is probably the one most evident in "self-made" people, those who started with little and overcame adversity to become successful.

The secret of success is to do the common things uncommonly well.
— John D. Rockefeller, Jr.

EFFICIENCY

An efficient person is organized. An efficient person gets things accomplished—on time. Efficiency is another aspect of taking control of your life. Without organization and planning, your life is manipulated by other people, or even by inanimate objects. You can prepare a super report, but if you can't find it when it's due, no one is going to give you the benefit of the doubt. Imagine how difficult it would be for an auto mechanic to repair a car if she couldn't find her tools, or consider the absolute need for organization in an operating room.

Just as you are learning to plan your career and family life, you can learn to organize your closet, your desk, your files, your kitchen, your garage, and practically anything else. Books have been written on the subject. Seminars and classes are available. You can even hire someone to come in and teach you how to get organized and how to keep things under control.

ETHICS

Ethics is another word for your conscience, your sense of right and wrong. Some things are obviously wrong (embezzling funds from your employer, for example), but in other areas, principles are less clear. If you learn that your best friend cheated on an important test, should you report this fact to the teacher? Talk to your friend about your feelings? Do nothing?

Standing up for your beliefs or doing what you believe to be right isn't easy or efficient, but it may be necessary. Without integrity or moral courage, the success you attain may be hollow and have less meaning.

This is one area of life over which you should have complete control. No one can force you to betray your conscience.

RECOGNIZING EXCELLENCE

We all know of individuals who exemplify these standards. Maybe it's a teacher you've had or a food server in the local café? Perhaps it's a public figure. Choose two people who you feel embody excellence and write them a thank you note, commenting on how they personify each of these six traits.

Going For It . . .
Work Is an Aggressive Act

In polite society, aggression is not acceptable behavior. At most parties, headlocks and half-nelsons are not appropriate forms of greeting. Those who attack the refreshment table in a flying wedge are unlikely to be invited back anytime soon. This will not come as news to most readers.

What *may* surprise you, though, is that aggression is *exactly* what it takes to succeed at work. Not aggression toward *people* (unless you happen to be a professional wrestler, a defensive lineman in the NFL, or the like), but aggression toward your work. Aggression takes many forms. It fuels competition as well as many other ways of behaving. Without some form of aggressive energy, we would probably never grow up.

How aggressive are you when you take on a job? Many people, especially women, find it difficult to identify with the term. It doesn't seem "nice" somehow. Wouldn't the world be a better place if everyone stifled their aggressive urges at work the same way they do at a party? Consider the following situations before you make up your mind.

SCENARIO 1
You are trapped in a burning house. The firefighters arrive, but the doors are locked. Would you prefer to have them

   a. wait patiently for a locksmith (the "nice" thing) or

   b. kick in the doors and windows and get you *out* of there (extremely aggressive behavior)?

SCENARIO 2
You are unjustly accused of a crime. During your trial, your lawyer uncovers evidence that proves your accuser is lying. Should your lawyer

   a. refuse to confront the witness because it wouldn't be polite or

   b. nail him to the wall?

SCENARIO 3
Your car won't start. You need to be at an important conference in an hour. When you call the repair shop, would you rather have the mechanic

   a. sympathize with your plight or

   b. be at your house within 10 minutes and have you on your way in 15?

SCENARIO 4
You are a doctor. You witness a traffic accident in which a child is seriously injured. Should you

   a. try to find out the name of the child's doctor and call him or her or

   b. do what is necessary to save the child's life?

SCENARIO 5
You are one of five junior executives in a small corporation. Each of you is asked to write a proposal for increasing sales. Should you

   a. be careful not to outdo your co-workers or

   b. do your best, for your own sake and the company's?

SCENARIO 6
You are a newspaper reporter who hears a rumor that, if true, could drastically affect the lives of many of your readers. Should you

   a. hope someone will call and tell you what's going on or

   b. investigate vigorously to either verify the story or prove it's not true?

In his book, *Work and Love: The Crucial Balance,* Dr. Jay B. Rohrlich points out that "the basic aggressive urge . . . underlies all work." Perhaps that helps explain the language people use when they talk about what they do. They *tackle* problems, *wrestle* with alternatives, *make a killing* in the stock market, and so on.

According to Dr. Rohrlich, "'Perfection,' 'greatness,' 'mastery,' and 'excellence' revolve around the instinct of aggression." And, as the exercise you just completed demonstrates, "people who fear and suppress their aggressive drives are usually unsuccessful at work."

The drive is there. Don't be afraid to use it. Try to recognize it and channel it consciously. Whether you are a poet or a firefighter, remember that aggression, properly used, will allow you to do your best work. To quote Dr. Rohrlich once more, aggression "is a constructive, creative, and adaptive drive, the fundamental aim of which is to foster the survival, preservation, and enrichment of ourselves and our communities."

So go for it! It's your life!

You're The Boss

Picture yourself as an employer. Your restaurant, "Chris's Creative Cuisine," has been the center of your world since you started it 16 years ago. For the first three years, you worked 12 or more hours a day, taking charge of everything from setting tables to testing recipes. You saw little of your children, unless your spouse brought them by the restaurant. The personal costs were high—perhaps too high. The business finally became profitable five years after you opened. Now "Chris's" is one of the most popular dining spots in town. Things are looking good, and you are determined to stay successful. It's time for the annual performance review of your employees. What advice would you give to the following people if they worked for you?

SHARON

Sharon is a good waitress. She is late for work several times a week, but she always has a good excuse. She apologizes and says it won't happen again. But it does. Last week, Tim, another waiter, had to serve clients at Sharon's tables in addition to his own for two and a half hours because Sharon's car had broken down. (She says it's in good shape now.) Tim said he didn't mind the extra work, but it bothered you.

What is Sharon's problem? _____

_____

What advice would you give her during her evaluation?

_____

_____

Write and diagram an objective that Sharon might use to change her behavior.

_____

_____

JACKIE

Jackie, your pastry chef, has won several awards for her dessert, Death by Chocolate. She has a tendency, though, to call in sick more often than seems likely. Even more unusual, her illnesses tend to occur on Saturday, your busiest day. Twice you've called her apartment to see how she's doing, but she wasn't home. When the mayor ate at "Chris's" last month, you were left with no desserts until Tim suggested an excellent bakery across town that delivers.

What is Jackie's problem? _____

What advice would you give her during her evaluation?

_____

_____

Write and diagram an objective that Jackie might use to change her behavior.

_____

_____

DOROTHY

Dorothy, your hostess, does a good job, but complains about other people's work a lot. She doesn't get along well with her fellow employees, and sometimes even lets her moodiness affect the way she treats customers. You recently overheard her make a rude remark to a long-time regular client and thought he'd never come back. Fortunately, though, Tim was able to make amends while he served dinner, and the client left smiling.

What is Dorothy's problem? _____

What advice would you give her during her evaluation?

_____

_____

Write and diagram an objective that Dorothy might use to change her behavior.

_____

_____

MAT

Mat is a busboy who would like to become a waiter. He does his job adequately—but no more than that. He usually has to be asked to refill water glasses or empty coffee cups. When a customer asked him for another basket of bread earlier tonight, Mat told him that wasn't his job. You can't help but remember the way Tim did the job when he started working for you.

What is Mat's problem?

_____

_____

_____

What advice would you give him during his evaluation?

_____

_____

_____

Write and diagram an objective that Mat might use to change his behavior.

_____

_____

_____

Unfortunately, we all encounter poor customer service on occasion. Write about three such events. How did it make you feel? What did you do about it? Did you tell your friends about it?

STUART

Stuart is a reliable waiter. He's never been late or missed a day of work. You've noticed, however, that since he started working for you, you've had to reorder things like candles and matchbooks more often than you did before. After a wedding reception at "Chris's" recently, you saw him walk off with the centerpiece from the bridal table. It's true that the flowers had been left, but Stuart didn't even ask. Tim had offered to deliver the flowers to patients at a nearby nursing home.

What is Stuart's problem?

_____

_____

_____

What advice would you give him during his evaluation?

_____

_____

_____

Write and diagram an objective that Stuart might use to change his behavior.

_____

_____

_____

TRAITS OF THOSE WHO GET AHEAD

Now that you've considered some less-than-perfect workers, can you describe a model employee? It might help to review the profiles above. If the characteristics described are undesirable, what opposite traits would make an employee valued by his or her employer?

Employee	Problem	Desired Behavior
Sharon	Tardiness	_____
Jackie	Untruthfulness	_____
Dorothy	Difficult Personality	_____
Stuart	Dishonesty	_____
Mat	Laziness	_____

What characteristic did Tim display in each of the situations?

_____

_____

Describe the characteristics of people you would like to hire for your business. Who do you want on your "team?"

_____

_____

Chances are your description is a fairly accurate definition of the term "work ethic." Being a good employee means being honest, on time, and so on. But the best employees—the ones who get ahead—display the traits that Tim does: they are creative, cooperative, and willing to do *more* than is expected of them. To many employers, a "good work habit" is more important in a prospective employee than knowing something about the job. They feel the job skills can always be learned. It's more difficult to instill the attitude they are seeking.

The work ethic *is* an attitude. The easiest way to acquire it is by liking what you do. Once again, it becomes apparent that, if you enjoy your work, you will do a good job. And, if you do a good job, you will succeed.

Interview three local employers to find out what they expect of their employees. Ask them to rank the characteristics they look for in order of importance. Would someone with each of those characteristics, but limited work experience, still be a good job candidate? Why? How important are character traits like honesty, dependability, punctuality, respect, and getting along with co-workers?

The Employee of the Twenty-first Century

It was a typical morning at the Millers. "Here's your juice, dear," Mrs. Miller said to her daughter, Angela. "Don't forget to take your cholesterol pill."

"I don't have time," Angela answered. "I'm late already, and I can't find my homework, my list of New Year's resolutions."

"I can't believe it's going to be 2040 in a few days," her mother said. "By the way, dear, you left the time machine on again last night. When your father came home, it was 1956 in here. You know how that always upsets him."

"Gee, I'm sorry, Mom. I was doing some research for my class in early television literature. I guess I just forgot to turn it off."

"I suppose you think you're the only one in the family who needs to travel in time," said her brother, Donald, as he came into the kitchen. "I was going to meet Herb and Joe in 1969 last night."

"Well, I certainly think my education is more important than your pleasure trips with your weird friends. Talk about a waste of time!"

"You see how selfish she is, Mom? I don't know why I can't have my own TM. Lots of other guys do. And I'm almost 16."

Like most stories about the future, the one above is almost certainly inaccurate. Chances are you won't have a personal time machine. You may never be beamed aboard the Starship Enterprise or travel back to the future in a souped-up Delorean.

However, you will live there (in the future, that is—not in the Delorean). You will spend all of your working life in the twenty-first century. And, if you bring along certain attitudes, you might just "live long and prosper."

Although detailed predictions about life in the years ahead are unreliable, it is quite possible to make an educated guess about the general direction of events. Certain trends are already apparent and are becoming stronger.

Most of these trends are related to technology and the ways in which it has made our world smaller. Advancing technology, of course, is nothing new, but its speed is. Thousands of years elapsed between the invention of the wheel and the invention of the automobile, but the first successful airplane left the ground only two-thirds of a century before people landed on the moon. Back in the 1950s, the first commercial computers were called "electronic brains" and were so big they filled an entire room. Because of their expense, only a few of the very largest corporations could afford to use them. Today, computers are as common as TV sets, and the Internet has revolutionized how we work, play, and live.

Because of advances like these, business has taken on a global perspective. Businesses from around the world work together—or compete against each other—to produce quality products and services at affordable prices. In order to do this, they have changed. The people who work for them have had to change, too.

How well will you function in this new environment? The following self-evaluation quiz should give you some idea. Select the answer that best describes or comes closest to your feelings.

1. I view computers as:
   ☐ a. an important tool.
   ☐ b. useful at times.
   ☐ c. ...I don't want anything to do with them.

2. If I need to learn a new procedure while working on a computer, I:
   ☐ a. figure it out after looking it up in the manual or online tutorial.
   ☐ b. get help from someone who knows what to do.
   ☐ c. give up—it takes too much time, and I didn't want to do it anyway.

3. I think of technology as:
   ☐ a. something we all need to know and understand.
   ☐ b. ...I don't think about it much.
   ☐ c. not very relevant to my life.

4. When I get my diploma at graduation, I'll probably think:
   ☐ a. this is really just the beginning of my education.
   ☐ b. about what I'm going to do now.
   ☐ c. thank goodness, no more school.

5. When I have a question about something, I:
   ☐ a. look up the answer on the Internet or call someone who should know.
   ☐ b. make a mental note to keep my eyes open for the answer.
   ☐ c. forget about it—it probably wasn't important anyway.

6. I think of change:
   ☐ a. as an opportunity.
   ☐ b. with caution.
   ☐ c. with resistance.

7. If, halfway through a project, it becomes apparent that my plan for completing it won't work, I would:
   ☐ a. rethink my plan and come up with a better one.
   ☐ b. worry about the project and hope to come up with a better plan someday.
   ☐ c. lose interest and scrap the project.

8. When I'm around people from other cultures:
   ☐ a. I appreciate their diversity.
   ☐ b. I'm curious—but cautious.
   ☐ c. ...I am uncomfortable with people who are not like me.

9. The idea of traveling to other countries:
   ☐ a. sounds exciting to me.
   ☐ b. is of some interest to me.
   ☐ c. does not interest me at all.

10. Learning at least one other language:
   ☐ a. is important for everyone.
   ☐ b. is probably a good idea.
   ☐ c. is unnecessary—I can get by speaking only English.

To score your self-evaluation, go back and give yourself 3 points for every "a" answer you checked, 2 points for every "b," and 1 point for every "c." If your total score is 26–30, you have the attitudes that will make you a valued employee in the twenty-first century. They include the following.

X EMBRACING TECHNOLOGY

Today, people at all job levels—from the loading dock to the executive suite—use a variety of technological accessories. From desktop computer to laptop, cell phone to iPhone to Android device, Kindle to iPad, the list seems to change constantly. These devices allow employees to be more productive and efficient. Individuals who capitalize on the power of technology are among the most valuable workers. They have the attitude that they can master new applications and look forward to the challenge.

X LIFELONG LOVE OF LEARNING

In a rapidly changing society, skills need to be updated frequently. There's always something new to learn. A love of learning will not only keep you employable, it will also enrich your life and make you feel a part of the advances taking place around you.

X FLEXIBLITY

It's been said, "Nothing is certain but change." How you deal with this fact can greatly affect your future. It's one thing to cope with change; prospering in the face of change is quite another. People who embrace change and can learn to live with some uncertainty are more likely to thrive in today's workplace. Jobs and whole industries change—or even become extinct—and the ability to change with them is critical. Whether you need to upgrade skills or find a new career, how you manage the change process impacts your success and, therefore, your future happiness.

X AN INTERNATIONAL PERSPECTIVE

With Disneyland in Tokyo, McDonald's in Moscow, and Coke in Beijing, it's easy to see that the world is becoming a much smaller place. Businesses around the world are entering a global marketplace. Nations are joining together for mutual economic advantage. At the same time, people are celebrating their cultural diversity. They are also traveling more and, quite commonly, they are living and working away from their homeland. For those who can appreciate other cultures and understand the different economic systems around the globe, the future holds endless opportunity.

Do you need an attitude adjustment? If your self-evaluation shows that you could use improvement in any of these areas, make plans now to do something proactive to change. Write some objectives that will help you in the spaces below. (Turn to pages 186–189 if you need to review the process.)

Elliot's objectives are as follows:

Technology:
1. Learn how to build my own website by next fall.
2. Find and follow two blogs about podcasting so I can create three podcasts for the environmental club at school.

Love of learning:
1. Read two books on the publishing industry this summer.
2. Improve my tennis game by googling "tennis instruction online" and asking Andre to coach me during the holiday break.

Flexibility:
1. Write three different endings for my short story and then choose the best one before handing it in.
2. Try to find a new summer job in a career field I'm interested in learning more about instead of going back to work at the supermarket.

International perspective:
1. Join the Russian club at school this term.
2. Make three new friends from different backgrounds or cultures by the end of the school year.

Your objectives:

Technology:

1. _____

2. _____

Love of learning:

1. _____

2. _____

Flexibility:

1. _____

2. _____

International perspective:

1. _____

2. _____

Managing Change

Today, not only do you need the right attitude about change, but you also need the skills to manage it. The best way to do this is to be prepared. Keep your personal portfolio and files updated with the following activities. Then, if companies are downsized, industries become obsolete, or jobs move offshore, you can shift plans and quickly change direction or careers.

Embracing Technology: Keep a running inventory of the equipment you've mastered and the software you've learned. You'll want to stay current on the new formats, even if you have to do it at home on your own time. If you still struggle with the notion of technology as a whole, turn to page 231 and develop affirmations that will help you change your attitude about this critical area of job performance.

Lifelong Love of Learning: Keep your professional skills current and add new ones whenever you have the opportunity. The list you've started (pages 44–48, 132, 150–155) will continue to grow as you get additional education and training. You'll want to update your list of skills periodically and add them to your resume. That way you'll always have a current version in the event a sudden employment change becomes necessary.

Flexibility: Conduct an annual audit of the "health" of your industry and specific job title. For example, is this a job that is growing in the number of positions available, or is technology making it obsolete? You'll find the most current information available online through United States government web sites. For instance, the *Occupational Outlook Handbook* online has a section that provides an overview of the expected growth for all of the major industries. This resource could help you gather data and better predict if your job/industry is stable or not. If you see changes coming because of societal, economic, or technological shifts (i.e., airlines encourage customers to book online rather than using a travel agent), start planning a career move before you get your pink slip.

Transferable Skills Chart: Using your updated skills list mentioned above, determine the skills you could transfer to careers with a more positive outlook for the future. You may even want to make a new list using a spreadsheet format. Along the left column list your skills. Along the top row list the careers you find appealing. Then, under each career title, check the skills that you already have that are also necessary for that new position. Finally, at the bottom of each column, make a list of the skills you still need to acquire for this new position. You'll find it helpful to brainstorm with mentors and people in that industry.

An International Perspective: Stay on top of what is happening in the rest of the world, especially as it relates to the economy and job security. Read industry magazines and journals and follow news channels on the radio, television, and online. Understanding how the international job market relates to our free enterprise system is crucial. For instance, a person no longer needs to move to another country to provide products and services for that nation. Working via phone and the Internet is a viable option for many around the globe. Major corporations in this country employ telemarketers and customer service representatives located in English-speaking countries halfway around the world.

You'll want to begin the above lists and the related research right away. That way, when the time comes to enter the workforce or change your career, you'll be secure in the fact that the job you've spent years preparing for is viable and in a growth segment of the ecomomy.

A Final Note on Attitude

A reporter was interviewing a woman who worked for a famous actress. "What do you think about your employer's enormous success?" he asked as she transferred a load of the celebrity's clothes from washer to dryer. "I'm really pleased that she found something to fall back on," came the reply. "Because she doesn't know beans about doing laundry."

In his book, *Up from Slavery,* Booker T. Washington said, "there is as much dignity in tilling a field as in writing a poem." And that, finally, is what attitude is all about. It makes little difference what you do. If you can find pleasure in a job, if you do it well and with pride, any task becomes noble.

I long to accomplish a great and noble task, but it is my chief duty to accomplish small tasks as if they were great and noble.
— Helen Keller

Whether we find pleasure in our work or whether we find it a bore depends entirely upon our mental attitude towards it, not upon the task itself.
— B.C. Forbes

Belly dancing is the only profession
where the beginner starts in the middle.
—Anonymous

We learn by doing.
—Aristotle

CHAPTER ELEVEN

Getting Experience

Finding your first job

This chapter outlines the steps you need to take to get that first job in your field. The same principles apply to any job search. Learn them well. You will use them throughout your life.

There are many excellent publications with more detailed information on resumes, job hunting, applications, and interviews. Ask your teacher or librarian for suggestions if you need more assistance in these areas or search the Internet for information and resources.

YOUR RESUME

A good way to start your job search is to write your resume. A resume (it rhymes with "yes, you may") is a summary of your abilities, education, and work experience. It introduces you to possible employers, who will use it to help decide whether you are qualified for a job. Writing it will help you define your skills and abilities, clarify your career aspirations, and present yourself well in job interviews.

A resume gives you an opportunity to present yourself in the best possible light. Everything you say must be true, of course, but you can include information that may not come out on an application form. If your resume makes you seem more creative, responsible, and energetic than other job applicants, it may lead to an interview with the employer. That is its most important purpose: a resume won't get you a job, but it can give you the opportunity to meet the employer in person. Final decisions about whom to hire are usually made then.

A resume should be no more than one or two pages long. Appearance is important. Format it neatly. Better yet, if you have access to a computer, print copies of your resume on a laser printer. These look very professional. In addition, it is easy to change or update your resume whenever you need to if the original document is stored on your hard drive or thumb drive.

Check your resume carefully to make sure there are no errors, misspellings, or typographical errors.

There are several acceptable resume styles, but the one most often used is the chronological resume. It should include the following parts:

1. **Your name, address, and phone number.** These should be clear, complete, and at the top of the page. Don't use abbreviations, titles (Mr., Ms.), or nicknames.

2. **Your job objective or goal.** Employers want to know what kind of work you are seeking. This statement will also help you decide what other information to include in your resume. As much as possible, the information in the resume should relate to your qualifications for the job you say you want.

3. **Your education.** If you are still in high school, list the school you are attending, along with the city and state, and note what grade you have completed. If you have attended other high schools, list them in reverse chronological order (start with the most recent school, and work your way back to the first one you attended). There is no need to list elementary or junior high schools.

    If you have attended college or had other training beyond high school, list these schools, along with the years you attended and any degrees, certificates, or licenses you have earned. If you have taken classes that relate to the job you want, list them as well. Include any skills learned or honors earned.

4. **Your work experience.** Include both paid and volunteer work in this category. Again, use reverse chronological order. Start with your current job, or the last one you held, and work your way back to your first job. Include the company name and the city and state in which it is located. Follow with your job title and the specific duties you performed on the job. Describe your duties with action words, such as "prepared," "delivered," and "collected." If applying for your first job, be sure to include volunteer work. If you have served in the military, list the branch and dates of service. Include any duties related to the job you seek and any awards you received. If you were honorably discharged, say so.

5. **Your skills and traits.** Employers don't really care what your favorite TV show is (unless you're applying for a job on that set) or how many cats you have (unless you want to work in a pet shop). In other words, use this category for any information that is relevant to the job you seek. Your hobby of rebuilding small engines is definitely of interest if you are applying for a job as a mechanic's helper. But if you want a sales job at the boutique, it may not be worth mentioning. Turn back to pages 27, 47, 48, and 132 and review your lists of strengths and skills. Some of these can be included here.

    You might also want to include any character traits that relate to doing well on the job, such as "like a challenge," "always on time," or "never missed a deadline." Review your responses on page 39 to trigger your thinking.

6. **Your references.** References are adults—not relatives—who can vouch for your honesty, responsibility, and so on. Think of several people who would give you a good reference and ask if you may include their names on your resume. Consider teachers, coaches, friends of your parents, parents of your friends, your minister, priest, or rabbi. Provide their names, addresses, and home phone numbers. Do not give a business phone number unless you have permission.

    Many people simply say "references available upon request" on their resume. This is perfectly acceptable, but you must still be prepared to provide the names if you are asked. So get permission and prepare your list even if you don't include it on your resume.

An example of a chronological resume is included below. Note again that, for this type of resume, education and work experience are listed in *reverse order*. That is, it starts by listing your most recent school or job and works backward to your first job or high school.

This resume is for a high school junior. Elena's long-term plan is to be a veterinarian.

Elena Lopez

1245 Calle Real
Los Angeles, CA 91000
(213) 555-1200

OBJECTIVE:	A part-time position feeding animals, cleaning kennels, exercising dogs.
EDUCATION:	Central High School graduation date: 2012
HONORS STUDENT:	Courses include biology, chemistry, geometry, algebra, computer science.
WORK EXPERIENCE:	
6/08–9/09	**RETAIL SALESPERSON**, Bonnie's Boutique, Los Angeles, California. Sold merchandise, created displays, unpacked and arranged new merchandise, advised customers.
PET EXPERIENCE and SKILLS:	
6/07–9/09	**PET TENDER**, Cared for neighborhood pets while owners were on vacation. Responsible for daily feeding and exercising. Cleaned litter boxes. Groomed long-haired pets.
PERSONAL:	Hobbies include raising tropical fish and breeding Siamese cats.
REFERENCES:	Available upon request.

Elena plans to send her resume to the local humane society as well as to boarding kennels, pet shops, and animal hospitals in her area. With it, she will include a cover letter, explaining why she wants the job. Although resumes are not directed to a specific person, cover letters should be. See the business letter format on page 159.

Use this page either to write a draft of a resume for yourself or format one on a computer, print it, and paste it here.

_____

_____

_____

_____

_____

_____

_____

_____

_____

_____

_____

_____

_____

_____

_____

_____

Finding a Job

The next step in getting your entry-level job is deciding where you want to work. Your first instinct is probably to check the want ads for openings that meet your requirements and abilities. That's fine. But don't be disappointed if the job you're looking for isn't listed. Most people don't find their jobs in the classifieds. Fortunately, there are other approaches.

If you do find a position that sounds promising, by all means apply for it. Read the ad carefully and follow instructions. If it asks you to call for an appointment, do so. More likely, the ad will instruct you to write a letter of application and/or send your resume.

You already know about the resume. In your cover letter or letter of application, identify the position you are applying for ("I am writing to apply for the job of messenger advertised in the December 3 issue of the *Daily Bugle*"). Be sure to include all the information requested in the ad. Be as specific as you can about your ability to meet the employer's requirements.

Keep your letter short and neat, and send it to the designated address. Quite often, want ads are "blind." That is, they do not tell you the name of the employer, but ask you to send your letter or resume to a box number. This, of course, makes it impossible to tell whether the job location is right for your career investigation. Applying for these jobs is good practice, but don't count on getting your job this way.

Most experts agree that the best way to get a job is to decide where you want to work, and then apply for a job there. If you want to be a doctor and there's only one hospital in town, it's not too hard to figure out where you should be looking for work.

But sometimes it's not that easy. There may be dozens—or even hundreds—of law firms, restaurants, or clothing stores in your area. Here are a few ways to narrow down the field:

1. **Consider the employer's reputation or your own feelings about the business.** Where do you like to buy clothes? That might be a good place to start, especially if you've become familiar with some of the people who work there already. What restaurants are considered top-notch? Could there be a better place to learn?

2. **Read the papers.** Note which companies are making news in your chosen field. Follow up with more research at the library, if necessary.

3. **Network.** Ask other people if they know of a good company in your field. See if they know someone now working in the career you hope to have some day. Don't be shy. Ask parents, teachers, friends, relatives—anyone who might be able to help.

4. Or . . .

. . . Conduct an Informational Interview

This is an excellent way to learn more about your chosen career as well as to find a job. Here's how it works:

Get the name of someone working at the job you eventually hope to hold. A personal recommendation is best, but if you can't find anyone who knows someone in this field, try another route. Check the phone book or call the Chamber of Commerce. Professional organizations or unions may be able to help. Use your imagination.

Then call and ask for an appointment. It's okay. People do this all the time. Simply say something like "Hello, my name is Bob Johnson. My uncle Ted said you might be willing to talk with me about your job as a radio announcer. Could I take half an hour of your time to ask some questions?"

There are a few rules to follow: Be on time. Dress neatly. Be polite. Don't stay longer than you said you would. Send a thank you note afterward.

It is not appropriate to ask for a job during an informational interview. You can, however, explain your situation and ask your interview subject whether he or she can suggest some placed where you might get the kind of experience you are seeking. You may get some leads. You might even be offered a job. Even if you aren't, you will have learned more about your prospective career.

Here are some questions you might use during your interview. Add some of your own.

How long have you had this job?

What kind of education or training did you need?

If you were still in school, would you do anything differently?

What advice would you give me about preparing for this career?

What advice would you give about working in this field?

What parts of the job do you find most enjoyable?

What do you like least about your job?

Do you have any plans for a career switch? If so, what would you like to do?

DEAN'S STORY

Dean didn't know anyone in his new city. Looking through connections on his college roommate's LinkedIn network, he located a mutual friend who lived a few miles away and had a job in the industry he wanted. He made a telephone call, set up an informational interview, and, before he knew it, he was offered the job of his dreams.

Job Applications

When you've completed your research, you will finally be ready to apply for a job. In most cases, you will be asked to fill out an application form. Every employer has its own form, but most ask for the same kinds of information.

You will usually complete your job application at the employment site. Be prepared to do it right. Neatness counts. Read each question carefully and think about your response before you begin to write. Crossed-out answers give a bad impression. It's also a good idea to bring your own pen—one with a fine point that does not drip or smear.

You will need to have a social security number for any job you get in the United States. Do you have yours? If not, apply for your card now. Call the social security office in your city or visit the Social Security Administration web site for information on how to do this and to locate the office nearest you.

You might also need to have your birth certificate in order to prove your age. If you don't have this document, you can get a certified copy from the Department of Health in the state where you were born. Google "vital records" and the state where you were born.

Some jobs might require a driver's license, as well. If you have one, bring it along. If you are under the legal working age in your state, you may also need to have a work permit. Ask your school counselor how to get one if you think you will need it.

Bring your resume along. Information on your education and work experience will certainly be needed. You might be asked to include your supervisor's name and phone number and your salary when listing previous employers. Be prepared to list your references, too.

Some forms ask for information you may not know offhand. Ask your parents for help if you don't remember any of the following:

Your mother's maiden (unmarried) name _____

Previous addresses if you've moved in recent years _____

Illnesses or health problems you've had _____

Dates of your last physical and/or vaccinations _____

Some other questions you should be prepared to answer include the following:

Do you have the legal right to work in the United States?   Yes   No
(If you are a U.S. citizen or have a work visa, answer yes.)

How will you get to and from work? _____

When are you available to work (days and hours)? _____

How many hours a week do you want to work? _____

What salary do you expect? _____

Have you served in the military?   Yes   No

Have you ever been convicted of a misdemeanor or felony?   Yes   No

Most forms ask you to sign and date your application before you turn it in to the employer. Your signature indicates that the information you have provided is true and complete. It also gives the employer the right to contact schools, former employers, or references to verify your answers.

My 10yearPlan.com

The Job Interview

The personal interview is usually the final step in the job hunting process. The decision to hire you—or not to hire you—will probably be based on the impression you make here. Give yourself every opportunity to succeed by following these suggestions:

1. Be on time. An interviewer who's been kept waiting for 15 minutes will already have serious doubts about your work habits.

2. Look good—but not flashy. The interviewer's first impression of you will be based on your appearance. Hair should be clean, combed, and off your face. Clean and trim your nails, too. Appropriate clothing means ties and jackets for men, skirted suits or dresses for women. Take it easy on the jewelry and cologne.

3. Look confident. Sit up straight. Speak clearly. Make eye contact with the interviewer. Keep in mind that few people actually *feel* confident while being judged by a total stranger. The interviewer knows this and will make some allowances. But this is one of those situations where it helps to *pretend* you feel confident. With practice, you'll begin to feel more at ease.

4. Be prepared. You can expect to be asked a number of questions. Take time to plan your answers before the interview. If possible, practice with a friend, taking turns being the applicant and the interviewer. Better yet, if your school has video equipment, see if you can have your practice interview taped. That way you can see for yourself how to improve your presentation.

It's also a good idea to convince yourself that you want this job more than anything else in the world. The interviewer will pick up on your confidence and enthusiasm, and that can only help you. Be prepared, too, to tell the employer what you can do for the company, how you will be of value.

CareerChoices.com

You might be asked some or all of the following questions. Write your answers here:

Why do you think you would be good at this job? _____

_____

How did you hear about this company? _____

Why do you want to work here? _____

_____

What classes are you taking in school? _____

_____

What is your favorite class? _____

What is your grade point average? _____

What are your strengths? _____

_____

What are your weaknesses? _____

_____

What are your hobbies? _____

What are your plans for the future? _____

_____

When would you be able to start working here? _____

How many hours a week could you work? _____

How would you get to and from work? _____

What salary would you need to earn? _____

Is there anything you'd like to ask me about the job? _____

_____

_____

Dealing with Rejection

No one likes to be rejected. But, at one time or another, everyone gets turned away. This is especially true in the working world. There may be dozens, or even hundreds, of applicants for a single job. Since all except one will be rejected, your chances of being in the larger group are extremely good.

Your first response, of course, will be to take it personally. This self-blame can be on either the micro ("if only I'd parted my hair on the other side") or the macro level ("I'll never get a job if I live to be 150"). It's fine to review your performance so you can make improvements in the future. But the fact that you didn't get the job has nothing to do with your worth as a person. Nor does it doom you to a life of failure.

The best way to deal with rejection is to brush off your ego and try again. If you truly want to work at the firm that has rejected you, apply again. Employers respect persistence. Apply for other jobs, as well. When you are hired, you will find your sense of self-worth miraculously restored. If you give up, however, you will have to keep living with the idea that you failed. And you didn't. You just didn't try long enough.

Until you get that job, though, here are some things that might help you feel better:

Seek out and spend time with people who make you feel good about yourself. Stay away from those who are quick to find fault with you.

Do something you're good at. Playing the piano or shooting baskets or writing a poem can help you remember that you have many talents and are a capable person.

Improve your job hunting skills. Practice your interview style.

Watch your favorite inspirational movie—one where the hero or heroine overcomes unbearable tragedy or unspeakable evil (and you thought you had problems!) to become the champion or the star or save the world. If he or she can do it, so can you. As Rocky Balboa once said, "Go for it!"

Accepting a Job

The day finally arrives—you are offered a job. What do you do now? Assuming that this is a job you want, there are still a few things to get straight. (If you have decided you don't want this job, thank the employer for the offer and explain that you have taken another position, you can't spare that much time away from your studies, or whatever. Don't burn any bridges, though. Don't say anything negative about the job or the employer. Even though you don't want to work there now, you might someday.)

Before you accept a job, make sure you clearly understand what it entails. What are your duties and responsibilities? When do you start? What days and hours will you work? Will you be expected to put in extra hours from time to time? Will you need a uniform? If so, where can you get one? Who will pay for it? How much will you earn, and how often will you be paid?

At higher levels, salaries are usually negotiable. Beginners, though, often must accept what they are offered if they want the job. Since the purpose of this job is to give you exposure to your chosen career, you probably won't want to make an issue of this.

However, if there is a salary range (say, from $7.25 an hour to $8.50 an hour) for people working at this job, you might practice your negotiating skills. Do you have any previous experience or special training that might entitle you to a salary at the higher end of the scale? If so, make your case. If you can't think of any reason why you should get the higher rate, it's best to accept the amount offered.

Making Connections

When you start working at your job, also start looking for mentors. One thing most successful people have in common is that, throughout their lives, they've had help from others. The word mentor means counselor or teacher. But employers or co-workers, parents, neighbors, coaches, and others can be mentors as well.

What do mentors do? Basically, they give you advice and encouragement. They "show you the ropes." If you've ever moved to a new school and found someone to tell you about different teachers and classes and advise you on what to wear, how to speak, and so forth, you've had a mentor.

Why are they important? For one thing, they save you time. Imagine how much longer it would take to learn the customs of a new school without advice: What is the one excuse you should *never* use with Ms. Bloom when your biology homework is late? What's the best thing to order in the cafeteria? Where do people go on Saturday night? When you go to work for a new company, a mentor can answer similar questions to help you feel comfortable and look competent.

Mentors are valuable sources of information. If they can't tell you what you need to know, they can often tell you where to look or who to ask. Because of their experience, they can teach you things you won't learn anywhere else. They can introduce you to other people in the company or in your field. They can help you become better known.

Best of all, mentors encourage you and push you to do your best. They applaud you when you do well. They build your confidence.

So where do you find them? Some people seem to know instinctively that they can benefit from these contacts, and have no problem recognizing potential mentors. Others haven't given the subject much thought. But it's not that difficult.

Teachers, coaches, and employers are the most obvious sources of help. Not surprisingly, the best way to get their attention is to do a good job. Teachers and coaches, especially, love their subject or sport and find great satisfaction in helping young people excel in their field. Similarly, employers are often more than willing to help promising employees learn their trade.

From time to time, you are likely to meet other people who could enrich your life. It's never a good idea—or proper behavior—to be a pest or to force your attentions on anyone. But most people are willing to answer a question or offer information. You can follow up with a thank you note. Perhaps a mentor relationship will develop. Perhaps not. Again, don't push it.

The best relationships develop naturally. If there's no friendship or rapport between two people, the association won't last.

We've talked about what a mentor can do for you. But what can you do for a mentor? Well, you can carry on in his or her tradition or trade. Better yet, you can continue the practice. As you establish yourself in your career, extend a hand to those who follow. Become a mentor yourself.

Can you think of people who have served as mentors for you in the past? List them below. What did they do that you found helpful?

_____

_____

_____

How about now? Are there potential or actual mentors in your life? List them here. How have they, or how could they, help you?

_____

_____

_____

_____

Think about the training or work you are currently planning to get or do in the next 10 years. What kinds of mentors do you need? List them by title or classification below.

_____

_____

_____

_____

Have you ever been a mentor? To whom? What did you do? How did you feel about it?

_____

_____

_____

_____

Even if you're on the right track, you'll get
run over if you just sit there.
—Will Rogers

CHAPTER TWELVE

Where Do You Go from Here?

Writing your 10-year plan

A journey of a thousand leagues begins
with a single step.

— Lao-tzu

Section Three:
HOW DO I GET IT?

We know what we are, but know not what we may be.

—William Shakespeare, *Hamlet*

They that would eat the fruit must climb the tree.

As we said in chapter 1, success depends largely on two factors: vision and energy. By now, if you have completed the exercises in this book, you should have a better understanding of who you are and what you want; you should have a vision. You have also learned a number of skills and techniques to help realize that vision, a task that required no small amount of energy. But, truthfully, your work is just beginning.

In this final chapter, you will write your own 10-year plan. You will think about and list the actions you need to take over the coming years to achieve your goals. While it may look like an overwhelming task, do your best to complete it because "if you don't know where you're going, you're likely to end up someplace else."

Your plan should be a flexible guide, though. Unexpected challenges and opportunities are sure to turn up, and you will need to adjust your plans accordingly.

Think of this chapter as a map. You know where you are. You know where you want to go. Your plan should serve as one route to your destination. You may decide to follow it all the way, or you may find an alternate path that suits you better. Perhaps you'll change your plans and head off in an entirely different direction.

That's fine, but make your decisions consciously. Have a reason for changing your mind. Then make a new plan, using this model if you like. Having a guide helps you remember your long-term goals and makes it easier to avoid actions that could keep you from reaching your goals.

Let's get started.

Sometimes, I think, the things we see
Are shadows of the things to be;
That what we plan we build . . .
— Phoebe Cary
Dreams and Realities

Getting the Education or Training You Need

Education is a companion which no misfortune can depress, no crime can destroy, no enemy can alienate, no despotism can enslave. At home a friend, abroad an introduction, in solitude a solace, and in society an ornament. It chastens vice, it guides virtue, it gives, at once, grace and government to genius.

— Joseph Addison

The things taught in schools and colleges are not an education, but the means of education.
— Ralph Waldo Emerson

A whale ship was my Yale College and my Harvard.
— Herman Melville,
Moby Dick

There are many ways to get the training and/or education you need. Most of them require one common thing—**a high school diploma**. You also need a high school degree to be eligible for most kinds of employment. Without this ticket to opportunity, you are likely to end up with a low-paying, dead-end job—or no job at all.

So stay in school. If you are having problems, talk with one of your teachers or counselors and arrange for extra help. If you've already dropped out and can't go back to school, contact your local school district about adult education or other options. You might be able to earn a GED or high school equivalency certificate.

After you have your diploma or certificate, you have a variety of choices:

COMMUNITY OR JUNIOR COLLEGES are two-year schools offering many advantages. They offer programs leading directly to employment. Credits may also be transferred to four-year schools. Tuition is generally low at community colleges, and, since there are so many of them (1,167), it's often possible to cut expenses even further by living at home. In addition, admission requirements are lower than at most four-year schools. So, if you didn't excel in high school, you have a chance to redeem yourself here. If you are interested in attending a particular school, visit its web site or drop them an email requesting admissions information. You can also visit the American Association of Community Colleges' web site at http://www.aacc.nche.edu.

FOUR-YEAR COLLEGES AND UNIVERSITIES come in all sizes and varieties. Some are small liberal arts schools that usually stress a broad, general education. Other colleges specialize in certain kinds of training. State colleges and universities are usually large institutions that offer both liberal arts and more directed studies. Some four-year schools are very expensive and/or hard to get into. Others are quite accessible. To learn more about them, check the library for guides such as *Peterson's Guide to Four Year Colleges*, or go online and google "college directories" for links to a variety of online resources. Visit http://www.careerchoices.com for links to comprehensive information on every college and university in the United States.

PUBLIC AND PRIVATE TECHNICAL SCHOOLS offer specialized training in a wide variety of careers. Attending one of these schools for a year or two can lead to jobs paying as much or more than many of those requiring college degrees. Like junior colleges, public technical schools usually offer low tuition and convenient locations.

APPRENTICESHIPS allow you to become a skilled worker through an arrangement between you and an employer, a union, and a school of some kind. According to the Department of Labor, more than 1,000 jobs can be mastered in this way. As an apprentice, you will spend part of your time on the job and part in the classroom. Usually, you will earn 40 to 60 percent of the normal wage while you are learning. Visit the Department of Labor's Bureau of Apprenticeship and Training web site,* or contact them for more information.

ON-THE-JOB TRAINING is available from many companies. It can take several different forms. You might receive instruction from fellow workers during and after work, you might be sent to classes elsewhere during the work week, or you might take classes on your own, with the company paying the tuition.

ONLINE OR DISTANCE LEARNING opportunities are becoming more and more prevalent in the post-secondary arena. For-profit along with traditional colleges and universities offer a variety of courses and majors to students who are self-directed learners. You'll find detailed information online. Consult with a career counselor to find the best match for you.

THE MILITARY offers both training for specific jobs and help with tuition once you are discharged. If you can get appointed to one of the military academies, you receive an excellent college education at no charge. (In return, you spend several years in the service after you graduate.) For more information, contact your local recruiters.

Ask your teacher, counselor, or librarian to help you find sources on any of these options. Extensive information is available at your library and online. Before making your decision, you may also want to interview someone who has attended the school you are considering, or who has taken the path that appeals to you most (been an apprentice, served in the military, or whatever).

What Is Your Commitment to Your Education?

On page 177 you indicated the career for which you want to prepare. Write that job title in the space below.

_____

How much education and/or training will you need to complete before you can get an entry-level job in this field? If you haven't already, update your *Career Interest Survey* on pages 150–151 for this particular career?

EDUCATION or TRAINING	DURATION
_____	_____
_____	_____
_____	_____
_____	_____
	Total _____

Use the information above to determine how many more years of formal education or training you need. Enter that number below.

_____ years

What educational requirements must you meet during each of those years (classes you need to take, grades you must maintain, and so forth)? List them on the following chart. What specialized training or skills do you need? Include this information as well.

Your Education and Training 10-Year Plan

HIGH SCHOOL

This year:

_____   _____
_____   _____

Next year:

_____   _____
_____   _____

The year after:

_____   _____
_____   _____

And on . . .

_____   _____
_____   _____

POST-HIGH SCHOOL

Year one:

_____   _____
_____   _____

Year two:

_____   _____
_____   _____

Year three:

_____   _____
_____   _____

Year four:

_____   _____
_____   _____

Year five:

_____   _____
_____   _____

Year six:

_____   _____
_____   _____

Year seven:

_____   _____
_____   _____

And on . . .

Life-long Learning Graph

Success generally depends upon knowing how long it takes to succeed.

— C. L. de Montesquieu

Nothing is so difficult but it may be won by industry.

— Terence

If you are planning to have a career that takes a great deal of education, the preceding exercise may have given you pause. Do you *really* want to spend that much time in school? Before you decide it's all too overwhelming, turn back to pages 114–119. Review the information there regarding the future dividends you can expect to earn for each year of education. Might it be worth the effort?

Remember, too, that although the investment of time may seem huge from your current perspective, you will earn the rewards over a lifetime.

Now that you have completed most of this book, rethink the chart from page 118, paying particular attention to the next 10 years. How do your initial thoughts relate to the training and preparation you need to reach your career goal? We have redesigned the chart to give you room to expand on your plans for the next 10–15 years. On each line, write your major activity for that year, whether it's education, training, or work opportunities.

You'll want to review the education and training alternatives you listed on pages 150–155 and 227, and consider a variety of scenarios you might substitute if circumstances dictate a change in plans. You don't want to give up your career goal if your preparation phase is interrupted. Outline a backup plan in the right-hand margin using pencil or make an extra copy of the chart for your portfolio.

Now add what you think may be your major activities in your 30s, 40s, 50s, and so on.

How will the next 10 years of preparation impact the balance of your life?

Lifespan Graph

90

80

70

60

50

40

30

High School
and
Grade School

29

28

27

26

25

24

23

22

21

20

19

18

17

16

15

10

0

Write your vision of each decade below.

_____

_____

_____

_____

_____

_____

_____

Write your Education and Professional Growth Plan for each of the next 10 to 15 years. It may be easiest to start at the bottom of the page and work your way up.

_____

_____

_____

_____

_____

_____

_____

_____

_____

_____

_____

_____

_____

_____

_____

_____

Self-Mastery Techniques

If getting the right amount of education was all you needed to have a satisfying and rewarding future, your path could be pretty straight-forward. However, your future also hinges on how well you manage yourself with all the other choices you make. You've learned self-control techniques for:

Delaying gratification
Facing fears and anxieties
Overcoming roadblocks and solving problems

You'll want to incorporate these strategies into your planning process, so you won't be tempted to scale back your goals and dreams as you complete your 10-year plan.

Delaying Gratification

Following a plan necessarily means delaying gratification. Turn to page 183 to review this concept. Admittedly, that's not always easy to do. It helps, though, if you are motivated and prepared. Answering the following questions should help you be both.

Can you think of sacrifices you might need to make in order to achieve your goal? Might you need to give up some social activities, for example? Will you have to spend some of the money you now use for clothes or recreation for tuition? List them below.

_____

_____

_____

_____

What commitments are you *willing to make?* (Will you study for a certain amount of time every day? Will you take a job to earn money for school?)

_____

_____

_____

_____

List the rewards you hope to gain from those commitments and sacrifices below.

_____

_____

_____

Do the rewards make the sacrifices and commitments seem worthwhile?

_____

_____

Turn back to page 121 and review the decision-making model on "the path of least resistance." Use it to complete the following statements.

Jodie's example: What do I want? *I want to be a lawyer.*

What are my choices right now? *To register for the advanced math class that will help me get into college and then law school, or to take the art class that would be more fun.*

I want to *be a lawyer,* **therefore, I will** *take the math class.*

What do I want? _____

What are my choices right now? _____

_____

_____

I want to _____ **, therefore, I will** _____.

Facing Fears and Anxieties

He has not learned the lesson of life who does not every day surmount a fear.
    — Ralph Waldo Emerson

My father, I remembered, had no fears at all. In that he differed greatly from me. But he could not be called a courageous man because he had no fears to overcome.
    — Yael Dayan

One of the best ways to overcome anxiety is to anticipate it, face it squarely, and take personal responsibility for overcoming it. Remember that courage doesn't mean being *without* fear. It means acting *in spite* of fear. It's natural to be afraid or apprehensive at times. But don't let your fears get in the way of your goals.

In the space below, anticipate your fears by listing every excuse you can think of for giving up your dream.

_____

_____

_____

_____

Now list every reason or excuse you can think of for not successfully completing the preparation or training you need to have the career you want.

_____

_____

_____

YOUR PLAN FOR OVERCOMING FEARS

Now that you've faced your fears, take responsibility for them. For each excuse listed above, write an affirmation that counters the fear and gives you power. (See chapter 10.)

_____

_____

_____

_____

They are able because they think they are able.
—Virgil

Experience shows that exceptions are as true as rules.
—Edith Ronald Mirrielees

YOUR PLAN FOR OVERCOMING
ROADBLOCKS AND SOLVING PROBLEMS

Just as you are responsible for overcoming your own fears, you must take responsibility for solving your own problems. Can you think of any roadblocks or detours that might get in the way of your success during the next 10 years? (Review pages 203–215.) List those possibilities below.

1. _____

2. _____

3. _____

4. _____

Imagine your life 15 years from now. What will it be like if one of these events actually occurs?

_____

_____

_____

_____

_____

Remember that you are in control of the situation. Can you think of things you can do now to avoid these problems? Write a goal and two objectives that will help you do that in the space below.

GOAL: _____

    Objective: _____

    _____

    Objective: _____

    _____

Your Action Plan for the Next 10 Years

> Fantasies are more than substitutes for unpleasant reality; they are also dress rehearsals; plans. All acts performed in the world begin in the imagination.
> — Barbara Grizzuti Harrison

> The secret of success is constancy to purpose.
> — Benjamin Disraeli

On the following pages, you will write a detailed action plan for the next 10 years. Before you begin, sit down and visualize your life over this period of time. (See page 217 on visualizations.) How old will you be in 10 years? What do you think you'll look like? How do you want to feel about yourself and about your life?

Your plan takes into account your education and training, living arrangements, employment, and finances for each year. You already have a detailed plan for your **education**. Turn back to page 271 for that information.

Your **living arrangements** include both *where* you live and with *whom* you live. Will you live with your parent(s)? In a dorm or apartment? Will you live alone or with a roommate? Do you think you will be married in 10 years? Will you buy a house? Use your imagination.

Think about your probable **employment**. Will you be working for pay? Part-time or full-time? At what point will you begin working in your chosen career? Will you need to take jobs just for the money while you continue your education?

Whether you are employed or not, you will need money (**finances**). Where will you get it? Will your parents support you? Will someone else? Do you think you might qualify for scholarships or financial aid? Or will you need to support yourself? How much money do you think you will need each year? Make an educated guess.

Your 10-Year Goal _____

_____

Once you have a clear picture of where you'd like to go and how you might get there, write your plans below. Word them as measurable objectives. See pages 186 to 190.

YEAR ONE — (Next Year)   Your age _____

Education and training: _____

Living arrangements: _____

Employment: _____

Finances: _____

YEAR TWO

Education and training: _____

Living arrangements: _____

Employment: _____

Finances: _____

YEAR THREE

Education and training: _____

Living arrangements: _____

Employment: _____

Finances: _____

YEAR FOUR

Education and training: _____

Living arrangements: _____

Employment: _____

Finances: _____

YEAR FIVE

Education and training: _____

Living arrangements: _____

Employment: _____

Finances: _____

YEAR SIX

Education and training: _____

Living arrangements: _____

Employment: _____

Finances: _____

YEAR SEVEN

Education and training: _____

Living arrangements: _____

Employment: _____

Finances: _____

YEAR EIGHT

Education and training: _____

Living arrangements: _____

Employment: _____

Finances: _____

YEAR NINE

Education and training: _____

Living arrangements: _____

Employment: _____

Finances: _____

YEAR TEN

Education and training: _____

Living arrangements: _____

Employment: _____

Finances: _____

My
10yearPlan
.com

To get it right, be born with luck or else make it. Never give up. Get the knack of getting people to help you and also pitch in yourself.

—Ruth Gordon

You know, when you're young and curious, people love to teach you.

—Dede Allen

SUPPORTERS OF MY PLAN

It's one thing to be responsible for your own actions, but quite another to feel you have to do everything on your own. Part of responsibility is knowing when to get help and where to get it. Review page 262 on the importance of mentors. Can you think of people in your life right now who could be of assistance in reaching your goals? If so, list them below. If not, start watching for these important people to turn up in your life. Whether or not you know any now, you are sure to meet others in the next few years. Learn to recognize them, and be open to the things they have to teach you.

_____

_____

_____

_____

In a world where there is so much to be done, I felt strongly impressed that there must be something for me to do.
— Dorothea Dix

If only I could so live and so serve the world that after me there should never again be birds in cages.
—Isak Dinesen

It is good to have an end to journey towards; but it is the journey that matters, in the end.
—Ursula K. LeGuin

MY MISSION IN LIFE

Back on page 61 you stated your mission in life. Is it still the same? Restate or rewrite it below and refer to it often. Although your mission may change, it will keep you on course. In the end, you are likely to judge your own success or failure according to how well you have lived up to this purpose.

_____

_____

_____

_____

_____

If your success is not on your own terms, if it looks good to the world but does not feel good in our heart, it is not success at all.
—Anna Quindlen

My **10yearPlan** .com

What happens next is pretty much up to you. If you apply enough energy to your vision, there is no reason why you won't someday be able to say, as Samuel Johnson did more than two hundred years ago, "I knew very well what I was undertaking, and very well how to do it, and have done it very well." Good luck!

Some people see things as they are and say "Why?"
I dream things that never were and say "Why not?"
— George Bernard Shaw

Hats off to the past; coats off to the future.
— American proverb

In the ordinary business of life, industry can do anything which genius can do, and very many things which it cannot.
— H. W. Beecher

Keep your eyes on the prize,
Hold on, hold on.
— Traditional Civil Rights Song

We are a success:
When we have lived well, laughed often and loved much.
When we gain the respect of intelligent people, and the love of children. When we fill a niche and accomplish a task. When we leave the world better than we found it, whether by an improved idea, a perfect poem or a rescued soul. We are successful if we never lack appreciation of earth's beauty or fail to express it. If we look for the best in others, and give the best we have.
— Robert Louis Stevenson

www.My10YearPlan.com

The cornerstone of your *Career Choices* experience is the development of a 10-year education, career, and life plan. My10yearPlan.com provides an online planning area where you can compile, store, and update the work and data related to the development of your 10-year plan. The online nature of My10yearPlan.com means you can have easy access to your plan for the duration of your time in school.

When you enter your information from the pages in your *Career Choices Workbook and Portfolio* that are marked with this logo, the computer program carries select information forward to create your 10-year plan summary page. This overview provides you with a snapshot of the goals and plans you've set for your education, finances, and lifestyle choices over the next decade.

As your personal goals change and grow throughout high school, you'll want to revisit and revise your plan using your own ID and password. This process will help you grow and maintain your vision of the future while empowering you to work the plan, stay the course, and realize your dreams.

1. Guttmacher Institute, *U.S. Teenage Pregnancy Statistics, National and State Trends and Trends by Race and Ethnicity,* updated September 2006.

2. Ibid.

3. National Campaign to Prevent Teen Pregnancy, *The Public Costs of Teen Childbearing,* 2006.

4. U.S. Census Bureau, Housing and Household Economic Statistics Division, Historical Poverty Tables, 2006.

5. U.S. Department of Labor, Bureau of Labor Statistics, "The Employment Situation: December 2007," January 4, 2008.

6. U.S. Department of Labor, Bureau of Labor Statistics, "A Profile of the Working Poor, 2004," May 2006.

7. U.S. Census Bureau, Current Population Survey, 2007 Annual Social and Economic Supplement, January 2008.

8. U.S. Census Bureau, Current Population Survey, 2007 Annual Social and Economic Supplement, August 2007.

9. Vice Admiral Richard H. Carmona, M.D., MPH, FACS, United States Surgeon General, in a speech entitled "Prevention and Treatment of Alcohol Abuse: Vision and Strategies" delivered at the National Medical Leaders Meeting, February 2004.

10. National Highway Traffic Safety Administration, "2006 Traffic Safety Annual Assessment – A Preview" DOT 810 791, July 2007.

11. National Highway Traffic Safety Administration, "Traffic Safety Facts 2005: Young Drivers."

12. U.S. Department of Health and Human Services, National Institutes of Health, National Institute on Drug Abuse, "2006 Monitoring the Future," December 2006.

ILLUSTRATIONS

Itoko Maeno—1, 2, 3, 4, 6–7, 8–9, 10–11, 12, 14, 18, 20–21, 22–23, 24–25, 26, 28, 30, 31, 32, 33, 36, 37, 38, 40, 42–43, 46, 47, 50–51, 52, 53, 54–55, 56, 58, 60, 64, 65, 69, 72–73, 74, 75, 76, 78, 85, 88, 90, 91, 92, 93, 96, 97, 98, 99, 103, 102, 104, 106, 110, 114–115, 119, 122–123, 124–125, 126, 128, 130, 131, 132, 133, 134, 138, 140–141, 142–143, 144, 146, 147, 148, 149, 150, 156, 157, 158, 159, 161, 162, 164, 166–167, 168–169, 174, 175, 176, 179, 180–181, 182, 185, 186, 187, 188, 189, 192–193, 194–195, 196, 200, 202, 203, 204, 205, 206, 208, 209, 210, 211, 213, 214, 215, 219, 223, 224–225, 228–229, 230, 232, 234, 235, 237, 238, 239, 241, 242, 245, 246–247, 248–249, 250, 252, 253, 255, 256, 258, 261, 264–265, 266, 268–269, 272, 275, 275, 276, 277, 278, 280, 281, 282, 283, 287.

Janice Blair—67, 71, 80, 95, 100, 101, 112, 113, 120, 121, 135, 136–137, 170, 171, 173, 199, 222, 240, 260, 263, 267, 270,

Diana Lackner—15–16, 44–45, 49, 62, 82–83, 87, 105, 107, 108, 109, 110, 183, 216, 218, 220, 285

*The art on page 202 has been published since 1990. We leave it as a tribute.

ACKNOWLEDGMENTS

We'd like to thank our peer reviewers for their important contributions to this work.

James C. Comiskey, Author and lecturer, *How to Start, Expand and Sell a Business* and *Successfully Self-Employed,* San Francisco, California.

Diana Frank, Community volunteer and philanthropist, homemaker, and designer, Goleta, California.

Rochelle Friedman, Ed.D., Principal, Murray High School, Charlottesville, Virginia. Career Vocational Education Administrator, Albemarle County Schools.

Kenneth B. Hoyt, Ph.D., University Distinguished Professor, Kansas State University.

Susan A. Neufeldt, Ph.D., Clinical Psychologist, Santa Barbara, California.

Laura Light, M.Ed., Reading Specialist/language arts teacher, Murray High School, Charlottesville, Virginia.

Carl E. Lindros, M.B.A., President, Santa Barbara Securities.

Sarah Lykken, M.Ed., National Sales Manager, Carlson Learning Corporation, Minneapolis, Minnesota.

Also special thanks to:

Christine Nolt, book design and production; Kelly Gajewski, editorial assistant; Janice Blair and Diana Lackner, illustration; Dick Rutan and Jeanna Yager for permission to use an image of the *Voyager* on the cover.

MINDY BINGHAM

To date as author or co-author, Mindy Bingham's titles have sold over two million copies. They include the best-selling *Choices: A Teen Woman's Journal for Self-awareness and Personal Planning,* and *Challenges,* the young man's version. Her children's picture books include the Ingram number-one bestseller, *Minou; My Way Sally,* the 1989 Ben Franklin Award winner; and *Berta Benz and the Motorwagen.* Mindy was the founder of nonprofit Advocacy Press in Santa Barbara, prior to founding Academic Innovations in 1990.

SANDY STRYKER

Sandy Stryker is co-author of the bestselling *Choices: A Teen Woman's Journal for Self-awareness and Personal Planning; Challenges: A Young Man's Journal for Self-awareness and Personal Planning; Changes: A Woman's Journal for Self-awareness and Personal Planning;* and *More Choices: A Strategic Planning Guide for Mixing Career and Family.* Her first children's book, *Tonia the Tree,* was the 1988 recipient of the merit award from the Friends of American Writers. She is co-author of *The World of Work Job Application File,* and has edited numerous other publications.

TANJA EASSON

As the National Director of Curriculum and Technical Support for Academic Innovations, Tanja has helped educators around the country initiate and expand their *Career Choices* programs. Her creativity and talent is evident in her work with author Mindy Bingham on the Internet enhancements CareerChoices.com, LifestyleMath.com, My10yearPlan.com and the online Teachers' Lounge.

ITOKO MAENO

Known for her sensitive and beautiful watercolors, Itoko's work has appeared in over 20 books. Born in Tokyo, where she received a bachelor's degree in graphic design, she has lived in the United States since 1982. Her refreshing style brings life to any text and offers the reader an oasis for contemplation.

Other books by Mindy Bingham and/or Sandy Stryker

Career Choices: A Guide for Teens and Young Adults: Who Am I? What Do I Want? How Do I Get It?, by Bingham and Stryker. 288 pages. Hardcover, ISBN 978-1-878787-41-1. Softcover, ISBN 978-1-878787-38-1.

Instructor's and Counselor's Guide for Career Choices, by Bingham, Stryker, Friedman, and Light. Softcover, 408 pages. ISBN 1-878787-11-X.

Workbook and Portfolio for Career Choices, by Bingham and Stryker. Softcover, 128 pages. ISBN 1-878787-08-X.

Possibilities: A Supplemental Anthology for Career Choices, edited by Goode, Bingham, and Mickey. Softcover, 288 pages. ISBN 1-878787-14-4.

Lifestyle Math: Your Financial Planning Portfolio, A Supplemental Mathematics Unit for Career Choices, by Bingham, Willhite, and Myers. Softcover, 112 pages. ISBN 1-878787-07-1.

Career Choices and Changes: A Guide for Discovering Who You Are, What You Want, and How to Get It, by Bingham and Stryker. Softcover, 304 pages. ISBN 1-878787-16-0.

Things Will Be Different for My Daughter: A Practical Guide to Building Her Self-Esteem and Self-Reliance, by Bingham and Stryker. Softcover. ISBN 0-14-024125-6.

Choices: A Teen Woman's Journal for Self-awareness and Personal Planning, Bingham, Edmondson, and Stryker. Softcover, 240 pages. ISBN 0-911655-22-0.

Challenges: A Young Man's Journal for Self-awareness and Personal Planning, by Bingham, Edmondson, and Stryker. Softcover, 240 pages. ISBN 0-911655-24-7.

More Choices: A Strategic Planning Guide for Mixing Career and Family, by Bingham and Stryker. Softcover, 240 pages. ISBN 0-911655-28-X.

Changes: A Woman's Journal for Self-awareness and Personal Planning, by Bingham, Stryker, and Edmondson. Softcover, 240 pages. ISBN 0-911655-40-9.

Instructor's Guide for Choices, Challenges, Changes, and More Choices, by Edmondson, Bingham, Stryker, et al. Softcover, 272 pages. ISBN 0-911655-04-2.

Mother Daughter Choices: A Handbook for the Coordinator, by Bingham, Quinn, and Sheehan. Softcover, 144 pages. ISBN 0-911655-44-1.

Women Helping Girls With Choices: A Handbook For Community Service Organizations, by Bingham and Stryker. Softcover, 192 pages. ISBN 0-911655-00-X.

All of the following children's full-color picture books are 9" x 12", hardcover with dust jacket and illustrations by nationally acclaimed artist Itoko Maeno.

Minou, by Mindy Bingham, 64 pages. ISBN 978-1-878787-88-0.

Tonia the Tree, by Stryker, 32 pages. Winner of the 1989 Friends of American Writers Merit Award. ISBN 0-911655-16-6.

My Way Sally, by Bingham, 48 pages. Winner of the 1989 Ben Franklin Award. ISBN 0-911655-27-1.

Berta Benz and the Motorwagen, by Bingham, 48 pages. ISBN 978-1-878787-91-0.

Mother Nature Nursery Rhymes, by Stryker and Bingham, 32 pages. ISBN 0-911655-01-8.

You can order these books directly from Academic Innovations. Call (800) 967-8016. Allow 3 to 4 weeks for delivery. For more information, visit www.academicinnovations.com.